# AN AMERICAN JOURNEY OF HOPE

Donald Johnstone Peck

# AN AMERICAN JOURNEY OF HOPE

## Perth Amboy-The Capital and Port City on Raritan Bay 1683-1790

DONALD JOHNSTONE PECK

With Illustrations by
FRANCIS J. McGINLEY

**Flying Camp Press**

An imprint of

AHP
American History Press

Franklin, Tennessee
Staunton, Virginia
(888) 521-1789
Visit us on the Internet at:
www.Americanhistorypress.com

ISBN 13: 978-1-939995-02-5
Library of Congress Control Number: 2013951763

Manufactured in the United States of America on acid-free paper.
This book meets all ANSI standards for archival quality.

# CONTENTS

# ACKNOWLEDGMENTS

I would like to acknowledge the following individuals who inspired my interest in the colonial history of Perth Amboy: Isabella Ellis Carter Peck, Gladys Estelle Peck Johnson, The Reverend Canon George H. Boyd, George M. Boyd, Esq., Alma Geist Cap, Anna L. Cladek, Gwendolyn M. Compton, Jack M. Dudas, Esq., Richard G. Durnin, Ph.D., John Kerry Dyke, Elizabeth Frelinghuysen, Loretta Galvin Lewis, Francis J. McGinley, Helen A. Pavlovsky, William S. Pavlovsky, Charles K. Paul, II, Willard Sterne Randall, Albert W. Seaman, Esq., and Joseph J. Truncer.

I also appreciate the encouragement of the following individuals: France-Aimee Beekman, Helen G. Brudner, Ph.D., Robert F. Currie, The Reverend Canon Matthew T.L. Corkern, James P. Egan, Frederick Frintrup, Wendy Kennedy, Doris B. Kersten and Stephen J. Russell.

My final acknowledgements are to my friends C. Robert Kochek, former English Department head at Perth Amboy High School and Christine A. Retz, former managing editor of Associated University Presses, who read the manuscript for accuracy, and to David E. Kane, the publisher, whose final editing is much appreciated.

Donald Johnstone Peck

# PREFACE

*"Life is not a 'brief candle.' It is a splendid torch that I want to make burn as brightly as possible before handing on to future generations."* - George Bernard Shaw

This book is dedicated to my father, Tyrus W. Peck Jr., who, through his maternal great grandfather was a direct descendent of Sir George Scott and Dr. John Johnstone, Proprietors of the Province of East Jersey. Since 1685 nine generations of our family have lived in Perth Amboy, New Jersey. When Kearny Avenue was cut through the Proprietary House and Bell estate properties, my grandfather Tyrus W. Peck Sr. had a new house built at 95 Kearny Avenue in 1907. This is where my father was born, and as a young child I also lived there.

My earliest recollections are of strolling with my grandfather up Kearny Avenue past the Proprietary House, in those days called the Westminster. My great-grandparents lived on Madison Avenue and my great-great-grandparents lived on Gordon Street. We are the descendants of a family that survived the terrible divisiveness caused by the American Revolution between Perth Amboy families. As with other families, we became a part of the great American experiment of political democracy living within a diverse society.

Perth Amboy is a national treasure. It has needed a book that would bring to light its important historical role from its early beginnings as a capital city to its unique place in the history of the state and nation. In interpreting the battle between the patriot and the Loyalist causes that changed our religious and political liberties and forms of self-government, many American towns have watched history unfold, but few have experienced as much firsthand as the city of Perth Amboy. Beloved by diverse generations of both old and new families, its history has the power to inform lives, make sense of the present, and help enlighten its citizens to make appropriate choices in the future.

It is common to think that all the important things in American history happened somewhere else – New England, Virginia, New York, or Philadelphia. This is especially true when there is little original physical evidence remaining to interpret or promote it. To the discerning eye of the historian, the undervalued colonial history of the historic district of Perth Amboy is its most valued commodity. "Things which once seemed everlasting— are changing all the time," Thomas Wolfe wrote, and he was right. But change doesn't have to mean loss. It can mean the rebirth and reuse of historic assets. Preserving and revitalizing historic treasures can create sustainable communities and healthy economies and help illuminate how suitable civic choices may be made by each generation to shape their future.

Walking through time and valuing the extraordinary legacy of the historic area buildings and sites, you can view almost 300 years of architectural styles and feel history envelope you. As we turn a corner we may find ourselves in another time and place, not simply strolling down a street, but walking in the shoes of those who lived in colonial America. In Perth Amboy the elements of American history and contemporary life come together in an exciting diverse lifestyle that captures the imagination.

It is usual to think of history not only as distant in time but also in geography. Yet many of the great figures who were part of the American struggle for independence were here at the capital, avowed patriots like George and Martha Washington, Benjamin Franklin, John Adams, Aaron Burr, Edward Rutledge, Richard Stockton, Hugh Mercer, James Monroe, John Marshall, Alexander Hamilton, Thomas Paine, William Alexander, Adam Stephen, Daniel Roberdeau, and Nathaniel Heard. They were articulating and defending radical ideas—representative government, liberty, equality, religious freedom, civil rights and responsibilities—and William Franklin's actions added fuel to the rebellious fire that was already burning. Here too were the well- equipped forces of Great Britain, the most powerful military empire in the world, with their Commander-in-Chief Sir William Howe, Lord Charles Cornwallis, James Grant, John Simcoe and American Loyalists William Franklin, Frederick Smyth, Stephen and Cortlandt Skinner.

Distinctive because of its Old World connections to heredity, aristocracies, feudal land systems, established churches, omnipotent governments and slavery, the society of colonial Perth Amboy in many ways found itself pitted against the forces that held forth the promise of plenty and a way of life that emphasized freedom and opportunity for all.

This is a story of how a relatively small number of people of diverse national and cultural backgrounds succeeded in building a new society in what had heretofore been a wilderness and how that society dealt with the threats to its very existence by rebelling against its mother country.

Donald Johnstone Peck
Old Stone Cottage
Fords, New Jersey
November 2, 2013

# FOREWORD

Why do so many people from Perth Amboy cherish its history? What is it about Perth Amboy's past that makes it so special? To begin with, this city has enjoyed a rich and diverse legacy for five centuries, starting with its inception in 1683 and continuing into modern times. That saga contains numerous fascinating and complex occurrences. Some of those can be told as short stories, each of which would hold its own weight. However, it is when all these events are combined in chronological order that our history becomes most intriguing, and a web of seemingly endless connections becomes evident.

More important, these historical accounts involve and touch countless generations of Americans, some of whom have an ancestral connection to Perth Amboy. That link not only includes descendants of our early colonists, but also all the different waves of people who have immigrated to Perth Amboy in more recent years. Perhaps what makes Perth Amboy most unique is the countless number of individuals who take pride in their city's heritage, keeping this amazing narrative alive. For all of us, our history is a matter of civic pride. Simply put, it is ours and we embrace it.

If you have studied Perth Amboy's history, or have been involved with its historical activities, then you already know the author of this book. For decades, Donald Johnstone Peck has been a driving force for the preservation of Perth Amboy history. From his years of devotion to the Proprietary House, up to his recent involvement with the Museums of Perth Amboy, our author lives and breathes the city's history. This book covers the fascinating timeframe that encompasses the first 107 years of Perth Amboy's story. Undoubtedly, Mr. Peck enjoys the city's past as much as we do, and his love of history is very apparent within this comprehensive account of Perth Amboy's earliest days.

John Kerry Dyke

The *Henry and Francis* at Sea

# DUNNOTTAR CASTLE and the HENRY AND FRANCIS

*"Suffering is a journey which has an end."* - Matthew Fox

In May 1685 Sir George Scott chartered the ship *Henry and Francis* of the city of Newcastle upon Tyne, England, a ship of 350 tons and 20 great guns. Such a ship would have been between 110 and 130 feet long with scant room for all the passengers, stores, and goods. Of the 200 brave men and women who set out to make the crossing to Scotland's first successful American colony, an estimated 70 perished while at sea.

Scott's expedition was the most ambitious and yet at the same time the most tragic. Many of his passengers were from the dungeons of Dunnottar Castle. Some of the most uncompromising Presbyterian Covenanters were persecuted in the Castle of Dunnottar, Stonehaven, Aberdeenshire, in 1685, to supplement the notorious Bass Rock prison outside Edinburgh. Dunnottar Castle stands on a stupendous, isolated rock projecting out from the coast and rising precipitously to a height of 160 feet. Inside it had all the facilities to torture prisoners.

Robert Wodrow, the author of *The History of the Sufferings of the Kirk of Scotland*, wrote: "At Dunnottar, a large company was thrust into a dark vault, full of mire, ankle deep and had but one window towards the sea. The walls, it seems, were a little decayed and some little air came in at the bottom of the vault and they used to one by one lie down on their belly, on the bottom of the vault, that they might have some of the fresh air. Several of them contracted a violent cold and dysentery. Some who tried to escape by the one window previously mentioned were beaten, bruised, bound and obliged to undergo various processes of torture. Many died or were sick and all of them [were] in a very loathsome condition."

It was from the Castle of Dunnottar prison and other prisons of Edinburgh, Glasgow, and Stirling that many of the passengers on the last of the four Scottish ships to sail for Perth Amboy originated between 1683 and 1685.

Dunnottar Castle

Many marched on foot from the prison to Leith, where the *Henry and Francis* was lying to receive them. Detained by several delays, they set sail on September 5, 1685. This particular date was a major hazard. The summer was over, the stormy autumn was starting, and it was not common practice to make the crossing westward in that part of the year.

## THE VOYAGE

The voyage was disastrous. The ship was badly ventilated, had insufficient fresh water, was almost unlit below decks, and reeked throughout with the stench of excrement, vomit, and bilge. Along with the seesaw motion of the sea, it also shuddered, darting from side to side in tandem with the motion of the sea. The main mast split in two, and there were days and nights on end of mountainous tempestuous seas. The noise, with the wind screaming through the rigging, the slamming of sails, the creaking of timbers and the eternal wash of saltwater thudding against the side or crashing over the bowsprit, alarmed the already frightened passengers of the *Henry and Francis* with terrifying persistence. The main occupation of the passengers soon became simple survival.

Sickness soon broke out, especially among those who had been prisoners in the great vault at Dunnottar. Jail fever—typhus, no doubt—added to the already unhealthy tone of the voyage, and the moaning of the sick could be heard throughout the ship. To add to this misery, the food was bad, causing an outbreak of ptomaine poisoning. It was not unusual for three or four dead bodies at a time to be thrown overboard daily. Evening prayers with the recitation of the Twenty-third Psalm and the singing of hymns began to double as a funeral service.

This voyage—accompanied by sorrow, sickness, and death—brought with it a strong strain of Scottish blood to mingle with that of the other exiles who have helped make this country what it has since become. After a melancholy passage of three months, with days of pitching, rolling, and swaying through storms and squalls, about 130 persons arrived in the tidewater capital of New Scotland—Perth Amboy—on December 7, 1685. At last they had limped into the safe harbor on the western shore of Raritan Bay.

With the voyage and long ordeal on the Atlantic Ocean now over, the emigrants' new life in East Jersey had just begun. Sadly, they were so reduced in strength that they could hardly walk to shore on their own. And we are told that the local people remained indifferent to the fate of these Presbyterian Covenanters. Overwhelmed with gratitude for their deliverance that no further vicissitude could shake, "What could now sustain them," commented one of their leaders, Archibald Riddle, "but the Spirit of God and His grace?"

The *Half Moon* moored at the mouth of the Raritan River between Perth Amboy and South Amboy

# EUROPEAN EXPLORATION and the SETTLEMENT OF PERTH AMBOY

*"If you wish to make an apple pie truly from scratch, you must first invent the universe."* - Carl Sagan

The first European settlers of Perth Amboy and other parts of New Jersey were the inheritors of a struggling merchant tradition. This had been set in motion as early as 1498 when Italian explorer John Cabot (Giovanni Caboto) had claimed the Jersey coast for King Henry VII of England. The Florentine Giovanni da Verrazano, who dropped anchor off Sandy Hook in his ship *La Dauphine* in the spring of 1524, followed Cabot's lead. Verrazano sailed by present day Perth Amboy, exploring the Raritan River and subsequently the Hudson River, for Francis I, the King of France. In 1525 Esteban Gomez also explored this coast for the king of Spain.

In 1609 Henry Hudson was engaged to sail the eighty-ton *Halve Maen* (*Half Moon*) westward by the great Dutch merchants of Amsterdam who had already established highly profitable business relations in the Far East under the auspices of the Dutch East India Company. He was searching for a Northwest Passage through North America, via either the Delaware or Noordt (now Hudson) Rivers, to Cathay (China).

Hudson's trip helped initiate the Dutch presence in New Jersey and New York, as the Dutch West India Company had been granted rights to develop and administer the new territory known as *Nieuw- Nederland*. It was not until the early nineteenth century that the Northwest Passage quest was finally laid to rest.

When Henry Hudson was exploring the coast of the New World between Sandy Hook and the entrance to the Noordt River, he sailed a short way up the Raritan River and named today's South River (Zuydt River) as he had named the present-day Hudson River the North River. It is Henry Hudson's first landing at Sandy Hook on September 4, 1609 of which we have a landing record.

There is no record that any of the men from the *Half Moon* went ashore at Perth Amboy, but we can be sure that they saw the red shale outcroppings along the shore, the visual evidence of exposed clay deposits. They would have also seen the dark-reddish sandy shore as it gave way to cobblestone-sized glacial rocks, as well as giant-sized boulders at the water's edge—reminders of the last glacial age. The beach would have been dotted with broken oyster shells, with softshell clams buried in the dark red sand, and bits of surf-smoothed green beach grass scattered about the shore.

Here along the Perth Amboy shore Hudson's men would have marveled at the huge shell banks of the indigenous residents—cones consisting of the shells of oysters, clams, and even periwinkles, some rising to a height of twenty feet. Since shells supplied the kind of wampum that they valued, these mounds could be called the waste product of one of Perth Amboy's earliest forms of manufacture.

Unknown to these early explorers was the historic background of Perth Amboy's unique topography. During the Pleistocene epoch of the Ice Age, the most recent geological event to alter New Jersey's topography was the Wisconsin ice advance, which began about 80,000 years ago. During this period the ice was between 2,500 and 3,500 feet thick.

As the great ice sheet moved southward from what is now northern Canada, the leading edge of the glacier acted like a giant bulldozer, pushing and scraping the ground in front of it. As it advanced, huge boulders became rounded from friction and contact as they rolled along on the bottom. Many of these "glacial erratics" may still be seen in city parks and on private properties in the vicinity of Perth Amboy.

The advancing ice pack finally slowed to a complete stop, terminating in an irregular line that stretched across north-central New Jersey. Its edge extended from Perth Amboy to Metuchen, north to Summit and west to Belvedere, leaving behind what is now called the Wisconsin terminal moraine, a wall of ice estimated to be 300 feet thick.

The Raritan River and Bay were nonexistent until the ice eventually melted and receded north about 10,000 years ago. Under the terminal moraine in Perth Amboy is the northeast tip of New Jersey's inner coastal plain, which began forming more than 100 million years ago, producing the sands, clays, and marls so common in the area.

This Wisconsin terminal moraine shaped the promontory that characterizes the city's boundaries between the Raritan River and the Arthur Kill, first named *Achter Col* (After Bay), by Henry Hudson in 1609 because it lay behind New York Bay. It would be this favorable location that would later attract the Proprietors of East Jersey to build their capital city, which became the first successful Scottish colony in the New World.

The 1639 "Manatus Map," probably drawn by *Nieuw-Nederland*'s first surveyor-general, Andries Huddle, clearly shows all of present- day Perth Amboy opposite *Staten Eylandt* (States Island). In 1655, Governor PeterStuyvesant claimed all of future New Jersey as part of his colonial province of *Nieuw-Nederland.*

The Dutch people who settled *Nieuw-Nederland* emigrated from a country where political and religious freedom were highly prized, popular education was nearly universal, and regard for law and order was held in high esteem. In the seventeenth century, the Dutch republic had become a sanctuary for persecuted Protestants from other countries, most notably the English Pilgrims who left Holland and sailed to Massachusetts aboard the ship *Mayflower* in 1620.

The point at the mouth of the Raritan River on which Perth Amboy is situated was first granted by the Lenape Indians on December 8, 1651, and is first mentioned in a deed to Augustine Herman, a Bohemian who had settled with the Dutch in *Nieuw-Nederland.* The word *Ompoge* (meaning "elbow" in the Lenape tongue) is mentioned in the deed, since it defined the promontory point as an elbow of land.

According to William A. Whitehead in his *Contributions to Early History of Perth Amboy and Adjoining Country with Sketches of Men and Events in New Jersey*

*During the Provincial Era,* in a subsequent deed to Bailey, Denton, and Watson in 1664, no particular name was given either to the point or country; but the next year, Bailey, on transferring his right to Philip Carteret, called the country "Arthur Cull, or *Emboyle*" – which in 1666 was written as *Amboyle.* The charter granted to the town of Woodbridge on June 10, 1669 specifically provides that Ambo Point be reserved for the lords proprietors.

The capitulation of *Nieuw-Nederland* occurred on Monday morning, September 8, 1664, when Petrus Stuyvesant, the sixth and last director, surrendered the city of New Amsterdam to the English, officially ending almost fifty years of Dutch dominion in North America.

New Jersey's official founding date was when it was invaded, not when it was actually founded. Nevertheless, this surrender did not mark the end of Dutch cultural influence, for the descendants of the original settlers lived much as they had before and, at least among themselves, continued to speak the Dutch language well into the nineteenth century.

Among Perth Amboy Dutch families interred and recorded in *The History of St. Peter's Church, Perth Amboy* are Bartow, Bloodgood, Conover, Coster, Hart, Hulse, Mandeville, Nevirus, Ten Eyck, Slaught, Tice, Van Brockel, Van Brunt, Van Dyke, Van Hook, Van Zandt and Woglom.

# THE PROPRIETORS' STORY:

## Perth Amboy as the Scottish Capital 1686-1702

*"A man has made at least a start on discovering the meaning of human life when he plants shade trees under which he knows full well he will never sit."* - D. Elton Trueblood

The story of how Perth Amboy came into being is in many ways the story of the regime of the twenty-four Proprietors of East Jersey. In March 1664, Stuart King Charles II of England gave his brother James, the Duke of York (later King James VII of Scotland and King James II of England) all of Dutch–occupied New Jersey. With lavish generosity, on June 23 and 24, 1664 James in turn granted what is now New Jersey to two close friends, Sir George Carteret and John, Lord Berkeley. June 23, 2014 marks the 350th anniversary of the founding of the area of land now known as New Jersey.

These two Proprietors had served the royal cause of restoration in England during the trying years of the Civil War and the Commonwealth. The Duke bestowed the name Nova Caesarea, or New Jersey, in sentimental gratitude. Carteret had stoutly defended the Isle of Jersey in the English Channel for the Royalists during the Civil War in 1649, which had temporarily unseated the Stuarts from the English throne.

On February 10, 1665, Carteret and Berkeley chose Philip Carteret, a fourth cousin of Sir George Carteret, to be their New Jersey resident governor. Several years later, on July 1, 1676, New Jersey was divided into East and West Jersey.

The Proprietors—Berkeley for West Jersey and Carteret for East Jersey—had extensive and exclusive powers. Except for certain restrictions in their individual charters, these men were given authority almost as great as the king over their provinces. They could appoint public officials, create courts, issue laws, and impose customs, dues and regulations. Most importantly, they owned the land and could sell it, lease it, or collect quit-rents or fees from its occupants.

## THE TWENTY-FOUR PROPRIETORS

In order to pay the debts left after the death of Sir George Carteret, who died on January 14, 1680, his widow Lady Elizabeth, after whom the city of Elizabeth, New Jersey is named, sold the Province of East Jersey for £3,400 at the beginning of February 1682. According to author John E. Pomfret, "The purchasers were William Penn, gentleman, of Wormingham, Sussex and eleven English associates; Robert West, a lawyer of Middle Temple; Thomas Rudyard, gentleman and lawyer of London; Samuel Groom, mariner, of Stepney, Middlesex; Thomas Hart, merchant, of Enfield, Middlesex; Richard Mew, baker, of Middlesex; Ambrose Rigge, gentleman, of Gatton Place, Surrey; John Heywood, citizen and upholsterer of London; Hugh Hartshorne, citizen and upholsterer of London; and Thomas Wilcox, a goldsmith of London." With the exception of Robert West, all were members of the Religious Society of Friends (Quakers).

Again, according to Pomfret,

> *Before William Penn left for America in August 1682, the twelve associates agreed to take in twelve more, to make up the number of proprietors to twenty-four. Since Wilcox had sold his share, there were eleven old proprietors and thirteen new ones. The new proprietors consisted of five London men, all Quakers; two Dublin men, both Quakers; and six Scots, three of whom were Quakers.*
>
> *The London men were Edward Byllynge, gentleman and brewer, of Westminster and chief proprietor of West Jersey, now solvent again; William Gibson, Citizen and haberdasher and a prominent Quaker*

> *minister; Thomas Barker, merchant; Gawen Lawrie, merchant; and James Brain, son-in-law of Groom, and a merchant. Robert Turner and Thomas Warne of Dublin were merchants.*
>
> *The Scots were Robert Barclay, the great Quaker apologist; his younger brother, David; his uncle, Robert Gordon, a merchant of Cluny; Arent Sonmans, the Dutch-born Quaker merchant of Wallingford; and two noblemen, James Drummond, Earl of Perth, and his brother, the Honorable John Drummond, later Viscount Melfort of Cluny.*

On March 14, 1683, James, Duke of York, issued a new patent to the twenty-four Proprietors. Groom and Lawrie both have streets in Perth Amboy named in their honor. Thus was launched one of the most unusual colonization episodes in North American and Scottish history.

## WILLIAM PENN

The most prominent of the non-Scot proprietors was William Penn. After his arrival in America in 1682 he visited both West and East Jersey the following year. When he first visited Perth Amboy, William Penn described it as the "garden on the earth most like to Paradise." At one time he had seriously considered establishing his "City of Brotherly Love" in Perth Amboy, but he founded it instead as Philadelphia in 1682. Pennsylvania or "Penn's Woods" is named in his honor.

Penn owned vast tracts of East Jersey land bordering the Millstone River and near the Province Division Line. He also owned town lots and town land in Perth Amboy to which he was entitled. Penn Street in Perth Amboy is named in his honor. It is interesting to note that the principal streets of both Perth Amboy and Philadelphia have the same names, High and Market.

## ROBERT BARCLAY

According to one account, Robert Barclay, "...in September of 1682, was by the unanimous choice of the Earls of Perth and Melfort, with his colleagues appointed for life first governor of East Jersey, without the requirement of residence in the province." He was given the authority to nominate his deputy Thomas Rudyard, Esq. (1640-92), a Quaker who served as deputy-governor from 1682 to 1684. Rudyard was an attorney for the London Society of Friends (Quakers) and personal counsel for William Penn. He was also a direct descendant of King Edward III.

Robert Barclay (1648-92) was one of the principal leaders of seventeenth-century Quakerism and a man of great moral respectability. By the age of 30 he was considered the most prominent Quaker apologist of his day, and his book *Apology for the True Christian Divinity* (1676) could be found in almost every Quaker home in America.

Barclay's biographer, D. Elton Trueblood, credits Barclay for having saved Quakerism from extinction. The *Apology* is composed of fifteen principles which seek to offer a rational and theological justification for early Quaker beliefs and practice. It has been in continuous print by Quakers to this day. Barclay Street in Perth Amboy is named in his honor.

Robert and his father, David Barclay promoted East Jersey to nearby lowland Scots in the Aberdeenshire area. Four shiploads of friends and neighbors sailed from the geographic area north of Edinburgh to Perth Amboy, East Jersey to colonize and establish plantations. Many of them were Quakers.

The governorship of East Jersey presented Barclay the opportunity to realize his vision—the establishment of a colony for persecuted Scottish Quakers as well as the evangelical Presbyterian Scotch Covenanters from Edinburgh, Montrose, Aberdeen, and Kelso. This was in accordance with the Quaker plan to help the oppressed and suffering, to rescue prisoners and exiles, and provide them with religious liberty and toleration. West Jersey, which was composed largely of Quakers, did the same. These Covenanters of Scotland were much persecuted under Charles II, who attempted to force them to conform to the beliefs of the Church of England.

Between 1683 and 1688 Perth Amboy was the port of entry for both Quaker and Calvinist Scottish Nonconformists, many serving their terms as indentured servants, or otherwise arriving as rescued prisoners and exiles.

# RESIDENT DEPUTY-GOVERNOR THOMAS RUDYARD

Shortly after his arrival, Thomas Rudyard wrote:

> *Upon our view and survey of Amboy Point we find it extraordinary well situated for a great town or city beyond expectation. At low water round about the point are oysters of two kinds, small as English and others two or three mouthfuls, exceedingly good for roasting and stewing. The Point is good, lively land, ten in some places and twenty foot above the watermark. About it are several coves where many vessels may lay up conveniently; besides great ships of any burthen may all ride before the town land locked against all winds; the Raritan River runs up or rather down 50 for larger, some say 100 miles for small boats. There is also a healthy whaling industry along the coast and in the waters of Raritan Bay that a community located on this site could both service and benefit from.*

In May 1683 Rudyard sent a report to the Scottish Proprietors stating that three houses had been raised in Amboy, each measuring thirty feet by eighteen feet, substantial structures for their time. Stone was available for construction after a short sail up the Raritan River, and the Raritan Bay oyster banks were enormous and the lime from their shells was mixed with sand to make mortar. Rudyard's Surveyor General, Samuel Groom, also a Quaker, had surveyed 150 lots at Amboy as instructed, and houses were subsequently built on many of these properties.

# THE FOUNDING OF PERTH AMBOY

Officially founded in November 23, 1683 by the Proprietors of East Jersey, Perth Amboy was described in a report by one of them as a "... sweet, wholesome and delightful place proper for trade, being likewise accommodated with a navigable river and fresh water, and hath, by many persons of the greatest experience and best judgment, been approved for the goodness of the air, soil, and situation."

Named for James Drummond, the Earl of Perth, Scotland, Perth Amboy became the home of the proprietary leaders, the headquarters of the Board of Proprietors and the capital of the first successful Scottish Colony in the New World administered by Scots. As the designated Capital of East Jersey between 1686 and 1702, it later became the twin Capital of the Royal Province of New Jersey from 1702-76.

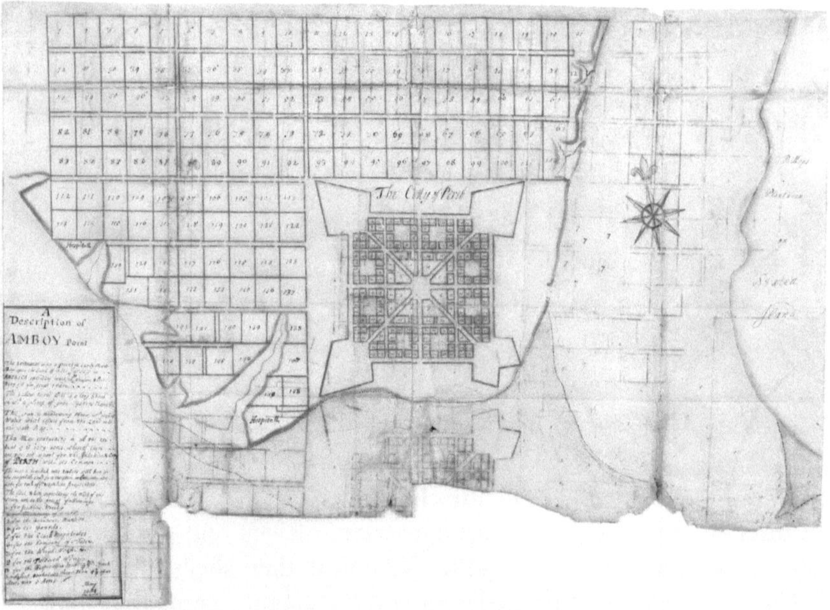


Barclay's Survey Map

# BARCLAY'S SURVEY MAP AND THE SETTLEMENT OF PERTH AMBOY

"Ambo Point" was chosen because of its location, its suitable harbor, and its convenience for commerce. Governor Robert Barclay caused a survey map of the capital to be made in 1684, and this survey map is considered significant because of its extreme importance in understanding Perth Amboy and the role the city played in the development of East Jersey. The Proprietary House Association owns a copy of this map. Laid out on about 200 acres of Ambo Point, almost as many acres of salt marsh located three miles up the Raritan River were set aside as a common pasture for the settlers.

A survey of the harbor from Amboy to Sandy Hook revealed a "broad and bold channel" and ships found safe anchorage even during "the hard frost" of winter. By 1683 a "convenient town for merchandise, trade, and fishery" had made its start on Ambo Point. By 1686 it had developed enough to become the provincial capital of East Jersey. Perth Amboy has been called America's first planned community because Barclay's survey map was the first known plan of an American city drawn up in the New World.

Today one can still see the evidence of the pattern of the streets and property lots of the Proprietors since the historic district of old urban Perth Amboy still follows Barclay's original survey map. It was a practical open grid plan of streets, with public places, a public wharf, and 150 spacious town lots, all positioned around a large central marketplace.

The market square was laid out at the intersection of the town's two principal streets, High and Market. Originally vendors sold their produce in the open air, but by 1740 the city had erected a permanent market house.

The Native Americans, the Lenni Lenape, called Amboy Point *Ompo* or *Ompoye*. This soon became anglicized to Ambo or Amboy on the English speaking tongues of the Scottish settlers. The town was also variously called New Perth, Perth Town or Amboy Perth. The town was first referred to as Perth Amboy in 1692. The name "Amboy" was so fixed in the minds of the earlier settlers that they named all roads leading to it Amboy. There is Amboy Road that crosses Staten Island to the old Tottenville ferry. Another leads from Metuchen and still another leads from Woodbridge. Other roads south of the Raritan River also share the name.

There were two ferries, one of which was the Perth Amboy-Tottenville Ferry established in the early 1700s, that was located at the foot of South Dock Street, now Fayette Street. It was the second ferry service established to take travelers to New York. The first had been established in 1669 at Communipau in Jersey City, with service to New Amsterdam. The other early Perth Amboy ferry, established in 1684, was the Long Ferry at the foot of High Street, with service to South Amboy and Lawrie's Road to Burlington.

A later ferry service from Perth Amboy to Staten Island was established in 1863 at the foot of Smith Street, at one time the site of the Town or Public Wharf, the oldest and most important of several wharves which jutted out into the Arthur Kill. The 1863 ferry slip at the foot of Smith Street was restored in the 1990s and is now a city-owned maritime museum.

The twenty-four Proprietors envisioned the erection of a great seaport and issued specific initial instructions. Twenty-four houses were to be built, one for each proprietor and an additional house for the governor. The purchaser of each was bound to build a house on it and was to hold three acres of upland with it as a nearby farm.

Additional large plantation landholdings were situated up and down the Raritan and Millstone River valleys and in Monmouth County. Estates of more than one thousand acres were not uncommon. A good example of this was the title to the land conveyed to East Jersey Proprietors Dr. John Johnstone and George Willocks of Perth Amboy, whose grant of some 11,000 acres would be known as the "Peapack Patent" of 1701, the foundation of most of the land titles in Bedminster, Peapack, and Gladstone since that time.

Many of these huge tracts belonged to absentee proprietors who either leased their holdings or merely kept them for speculation. Thus the basis was laid out for a sharp economic cleavage between the yeoman farmers and the landed aristocrats. The dual character of the land system—the small holdings of the townspeople in contrast to the large estates of the proprietors—has long exerted an influence on the economy and society of the colony and the state.

# PROPRIETARY GOVERNANCE

## RESIDENT DEPUTY-GOVERNOR GAWEN LAWRIE

Gawen Lawrie, a Quaker Scot, received his deputy-governor's commission and instructions July 1683. These stipulated that a division line between East and West Jersey should be surveyed and a road laid out between Perth Amboy and Burlington, the West Jersey capital. This road, known as Lawrie's Road, still exists in the form of Washington Road from South Amboy through South River, Cranbury and on to Burlington. The instructions also included "It is not to be forgotten that, as soon as can be, weekly markets and fairs at fit seasons be appointed at Perth-town."

The burden of the physical building Perth Amboy fell to Lawrie, including the houses for the resident proprietors and a more commodious house for the governor. Construction of the governor's house is thought to have begun as early as 1684, and it became known as Edinborough Castle. It was a stone brick-faced building 66 feet long by 18 feet wide. It stood just behind today's existing house at 225 High Street.

Having had a very difficult time with the inhabitants and their elected representatives, the proprietors removed Lawrie as governor in September 1686. Lawrie Street in Perth Amboy is named in his honor. George Keith, Surveyor General from 1685 to 1688, replaced him.

## RESIDENT DEPUTY-GOVERNOR GEORGE KEITH

The Reverend George Keith was born in 1638 in Peterhead, Aberdeenshire, Scotland and received his Master of Arts degree from the University of Aberdeen. He grew up as a Presbyterian but as a young man he became a member of the Religious Society of Friends. Until he left for America, Keith had been repeatedly imprisoned for his religious convictions.

Keith first came to Philadelphia in 1682 and then moved with his family to Perth Amboy in 1685. He was Surveyor General of New Jersey between 1685 and 1688. In 1687 he ran the division line, known as Keith's Line, between East and West Jersey.

An outspoken man, Keith was seen by Quakers as being too overbearing and opinionated, and with as many supporters as enemies. This led to his being excommunicated both in America and in England. Keith then sought orders in the Church of England and was ordained by the Bishop of London, in March 1702.

Keith's knowledge of America, his zeal, force and enthusiasm as a Quaker convert, and his association with a large body of dissatisfied Quakers in America led the infant Missionary Society of the Propagation of the Gospel in Foreign Parts, familiarly called the S.P.G., to commission Keith to make a general survey of the conditions of the church in America under their auspices and as their missionary.

Keith, who for two years or more had made Perth Amboy his headquarters, where he ministered to the Anglicans of Perth Amboy, became the first general missionary of the Anglican Church in America, traveling from New Hampshire to the Carolinas.

# RESIDENT GOVERNOR ANDREW HAMILTON

Andrew Hamilton of Edinburgh, Scotland was a great figure in East Jersey during the remainder of the proprietary period. In 1687 he became Deputy-Governor of East Jersey during the absence of Deputy-Governor Lord Neil Campbell. In 1692 Hamilton was appointed Governor of East and West Jersey, and was the first with his title to live in the Governor's House at Perth Amboy. Under his administration the proprietors' right to govern was called into question along with that of the Royal Province of New York regarding East Jersey's right to free trade, navigation, or free ports. The collection of customs was the major issue and New York won out.

Andrew Hamilton merits attention as the architect of an early postal system in America. Appointed by Thomas Neale, Master of the Mint, in 1692 to be his Deputy-Postmaster, this New Jersey governor persuaded the assemblies of five colonies to enact weekly mail services over major routes in New England and the Middle Colonies. The general post office was established in Philadelphia.

Hamilton died in Perth Amboy on April 20, 1703 while on a visit to see his family.

# THOMAS GORDON

Governor Andrew Hamilton's deputy secretary and registrar proprietor, Thomas Gordon of Pitlochie, Scotland, arrived in the Province of East Jersey in October 1684. The first recorded meeting of the East Jersey Board of Proprietors held on April 9, 1685, records that Thomas Gordon was in attendance. As deputy secretary it was his duty to record the acts of the Assembly and post them throughout the province.

Armed with issues of the province concerning supporting the militia, defending the frontier, customs duties, infrastructure, quitrent arrears, and court cases related to the land, at a meeting of the resident Board of Proprietors held in 1695, chairman Andrew Hamilton proposed that Thomas Gordon be sent to England to consult with the non-resident proprietors to urge their financial support. Gordon left for England in early 1696, where he remained for two years.

For thirty-eight years, commencing in 1684, Gordon lived in the city of Perth Amboy. W. Northley Jones describes Gordon as:

> *...a faithful communicant of St. Peter's Church (Anglican) and a charter vestryman. He gave a good part of the land on which the church is built. He was the first to be buried in St. Peter's Churchyard, in 1722. On the bicentenary of his death the Perth Amboy Caledonian Club erected a memorial tablet at St. Peter's Church noting his many offices: Assemblyman for Perth Amboy, High Sheriff of Middlesex County, Speaker of the House of Assembly, Attorney General, Treasurer and Chief Justice of the Supreme Court of New Jersey.*

Gordon Street, adjacent to the church, is named in his honor.

Historic burial grounds, such as St. Peter's Churchyard, are not only focal points for local history; they are important repositories of historical information and public art. The images that decorate grave markers—skulls, hourglasses, and crossed bones—speak to the brevity of life in colonial times. Early burial grounds, including St. Peter's Churchyard, were often racially segregated.

Some of the earliest surviving grave markers in New Jersey are to be found in Perth Amboy. One in particular is known to have been taken from Perth Amboy's old Burying ground established in 1684 and now the site of the Middle School on State Street. It was moved to St. Peter's Churchyard in 1876 and marks the final resting place of Helen, the first wife of Thomas Gordon. Her grave marker is dated 1687 and is similar in form and decoration to tombstones used in Scotland during this period. She, however, was not reinterred in St. Peter's Churchyard.

## JOHN HAMILTON

In 1707 the English government purchased the existing private post office monopoly, and under "The Act of Queen Anne 1710," which became effective on June 1, 1711, established a royal post office. Andrew Hamilton's son John was appointed as Deputy Postmaster General of America. John Hamilton was a communicant of St. Peter's Church, which stood on its present site from 1721 to 1850. Before that the lot held the ruins of David Mundie's 'Great Stone House,' which was built circa 1685 and was destroyed, probably by fire, sometime before 1718. The first post offices in New Jersey were in Perth Amboy and Burlington, located on the then direct route between New York and Philadelphia.

John Hamilton built his house in circa 1710 at 129 Water Street. Commodore Thomas Truxton later occupied it in the late eighteenth century. In the early nineteenth century it was the home of Captain Jacob Lewis, who distinguished himself in the War of 1812, and later served as a diplomat. His most famous guest in 1815 was Napoleon's brother, Joseph Bonaparte, the exiled King of Naples and Spain. Unfortunately this house was taken down in 1935 and replaced with the present Neo-colonial structure.

## A PORT CITY TO RIVAL LONDON

The East Jersey Proprietors envisioned the Port City of Perth Amboy to rival London both as a commercial port and as one of the great cities of the

New World. Despite its efforts to obtain recognition as a free port for various reasons, among them the conspicuous lack of a market for the merchants importing goods into East Jersey, it was always overshadowed by New York City. Sheer population may have been the reason. In 1698 New Jersey's population was only about 1,200 families. Perth Amboy's population was about 200 persons while the city of New York had 5,000 residents.

Although Perth Amboy experienced modest success as a port, it also lost business to New Brunswick. The major reason was the realization that heavily laden, smaller transoceanic ships could sail directly upriver to New Brunswick and Raritan Landing, saving time and expense incurred by loading and unloading cargo to and from smaller vessels at Perth Amboy for shipment upriver.

The proprietors' dream of a great port city that would be the London of the New World was never realized. The city seal visualizes this dream with its image of a ship riding at anchor in the harbor with the words *Portus Optimus*, or Port of Opportunity, below.

# THE BATTLE FOR RELIGIOUS FREEDOM

*"Much as I long to be out of here, I don't believe a single day has been wasted. What will come out of my time here it is too early to say. But something is bound to come out of it."*
- Dietrich Bonhoeffer

In his *History of St. Peter's Church* W. Northey Jones described Perth Amboy's early religious diversity:

> *Early Perth Amboy settlers consisted of Scottish Covenanters, many Quakers, and some English Roundheads—persons who feared the trend of religious affairs in their homeland, which was a decided drift toward Romanism fostered by King James VII of Scotland (who was also King James II of England) in 1685 on his accession to the thrones of Scotland and England. English Roundheads, in particular, were given this 'nickname' during the English Civil War because of their Puritan values of dressing, grooming modestly (and Congregationalist governance). They wore their hair short above their ears in contrast to the monarchists who wore long hair and dressed elaborately. Most sought to have a constitutional monarchy. England's many Puritans and Presbyterians were almost invariably Roundhead supporters, but as we will see not so in Scotland.*
>
> *The year 1685 saw the revocation of the Edict of Nantes by Louis XIV of France. French Huguenots (Calvinist Protestants) were finding their way here, as were Dutch settlers from New York. They were attracted to land and economic opportunities in Perth Amboy and the greater Raritan Valley. The next fifteen years saw the emigration of half a million of the French from France. Every seaport in America was receiving them.*

# THE PROTESTANT REFORMATION

The New World battle for religious freedom can trace its roots to the Protestant Reformation. The Reformation appealed to the urban middle and lower classes and to the peasants. The poor in the cities, and the peasants in particular, were in a desperate situation. They were ruthlessly exploited and deprived of traditional rights and privileges. As a consequence they were in a revolutionary mood that found expression in peasant uprisings.

The Gospel, according to Luther and Calvin, articulated their hopes and expectations as it had done for the slaves and laborers of early Christianity, and led the poor to seek justice. Luther reached out to these restive masses as other religious movements of an evangelical character had done before him. Both Luther's (1518) and Calvin's (1536) doctrines gave men independence in religious matters, depriving the Catholic Church of her authority. They are one source of the development of political and spiritual freedom in modern society; a development that, especially in Anglo-Saxon countries, is inseparably connected with the ideas of Puritanism.

Calvin's theology essentially shares the same spirit as Luther's did for his native Germany. Calvin's adherents in France, Holland, Scotland and England tended to be artisans and small businessmen. Unlike Luther, Calvin's central doctrine stressed predestination, the belief that salvation or damnation is not the result of anything good or bad one does in one's life. Calvin and his followers believed that they belonged to God's "chosen ones."

The outward signs of salvation placed emphasis on leading a moral and virtuous life. The virtues were: modesty and moderation (*sobrietas*), justice (*institia*) in the sense of everybody being given what is his due share, and piousness (*pietas*), which unites man with God. As a result of these efforts, success in worldly life is a sign of salvation, and failure was the sign of damnation.

The strong work ethic exhibited by Calvin's chosen ones was motivated not by external pressures but by an inner compulsion. This drive for relentless labor was a hallmark of the Protestant Reformed Church movement. It also emphasized the importance of human autonomy and dignity. These two aspects of freedom were interwoven in the theological doctrines of the

Reformation, and yet the individual remained subordinate to the purposes of an all-powerful state.

The Calvinist reformed churches of the Protestants protested against the authority of the pope in Rome over all Christians, and the belief that the Catholic liturgy used in worshipping God was the only correct way. The Bible took the place of the church as the final authority. The Protestant clergy's role is to help the people understand the Bible, but in the end each one must be free to interpret it as one wishes. Some Protestants choose to interpret the Bible literally, insisting on the letter of the law instead of the spirit of the law. To put it very simply, the pulpit replaced the altar. However, Protestants continue to recognize two sacraments in various forms, that of Baptism and the Holy Communion that they called "the Lord's Supper."

Among the Protestant patriots of the American Revolution, the processes of developing ideas of freedom saw the authority of the Catholic Church being replaced by that of the state, and that of the state by that of conscience. In America the successful revolutionary became a statesman, the unsuccessful one a criminal! These Patriots understood that all people do not worship God in the same way, if they worship at all, and that each person has the right to make his or her own choice. They understood that freedom of religion is one of the rights of free men and women.

Conscience held that all persons are born equal but they are also born different. This thesis implies that all share the same fundamental human qualities, that all share the same basic fate of human beings, that all have the same inalienable claim on freedom and happiness. It furthermore means that their relationship is one of solidarity, not one of domination or submission. What the concept of equality does not mean is that all are created alike.

## THE CHURCH OF SCOTLAND

The Presbyterian church in America can trace its roots to the Church of Scotland, which in turn developed from early Christianity in Scotland. However, the Scottish Reformation of 1581 principally shapes its current identity. In that year, in a movement led by John Knox and his followers, the Church of Scotland broke with the Church of Rome. It reformed its doctrines and government, drawing upon the principles of John Calvin.

During the seventeenth century the most evangelical members of this Scottish Presbyterian reform movement called themselves Covenanters. They derived their name from the Scots' interpretation of the word "covenant" as a band or legal document, expanding it to mean people who bound themselves to common action in religious matters. Some would add that the Reformation gave some Presbyterians a gruff side to their character.

## ONE MONARCH - KING JAMES I AND VI

The existence of the Kingdom of Great Britain began in 1603, when James VI, King of Scotland, succeeded his cousin Elizabeth I of England, and brought about the Union of Crowns. While Scotland and England continued as separate kingdoms, they shared one monarch, James VI of Scotland, also known as James I of England. It would take another hundred years of mistrust, terror and war between the two nations before the Union of Parliaments truly united them in 1707.

Since then, Scotland and England have formed one country in a political sense. But despite the centuries of union, Scotland is still autonomous, recognizable and distinct from all other nations. It is a small country roughly the size of South Carolina, and its population has remained more or less static at five million through the twentieth century.

During the reign of King James his subjects founded three colonies on the Eastern seaboard of North America: Virginia in 1607, Massachusetts in 1620, and Nova Scotia in 1624. The first two were English and the last Scottish; the first two survived and the third did not. The Scots left behind them the name Nova Scotia (New Scotland), which has been used ever since.

The Scots' efforts at colonization might have continued, but the following period proved to be the most troubled in their national history. By 1640 they were at war with England, after an offensive by Charles I of England to destroy Presbyterianism. The Covenanters—those who bound together to defend it—ruled Scotland for the next few years. During the English Civil

War the armies of Oliver Cromwell overran both England and Scotland, and ultimately King Charles I was beheaded.

## "THE KILLING TIMES"

Following the victory of the Royalists in the English Civil War and the subsequent defeat of Oliver Cromwell in 1660, the Stuart monarchy was restored to power. Englishmen summoned Charles II to the throne without requiring him to make any promises, commitments, or constitutional guarantees. King Charles II abrogated all acts from the Cromwellian period in favor of Presbyterianism, the religion of the vast majority of Scots, as opposed to forcing them to conform to the Church of England.

Under the Quaker Act of 1662, an Act of the Parliament of England requiring subjects to swear an oath of allegiance, more than 5,000 pacifist Quakers were imprisoned. The Conventicle Act of 1664 could punish by fine or imprisonment all those of any faith who attended meetings or "conventicles" of more than five persons, other than members of any one household, for "...any exercise of religion in other manner than is allowed by the liturgy or practice of the Church of England."

The brutal oppression showered on the Covenanters during the reign of Charles II, infamously known as the "Killing Times," contributed largely to the Scottish emigration of the Presbyterian Covenanters to East Jersey. For 28 years, from 1660 to 1688, they were hunted down, thrown into prison and sold as slaves. In addition, their property was taken from them and they were banished from the country, all because of their unbending religious beliefs. It is estimated that 18,000 Covenanters were either killed or banished during those horrible years.

## SIR GEORGE SCOTT

It was the vision of Sir George Scott of Pitlochie, who had been repeatedly fined and imprisoned by the Privy Council of Scotland for attending conventicles, to seek religious freedom in the New World. While Scottish emigrants settled later in North and South Carolina, the East Jersey settlement, with its capital at Perth Amboy, as previously mentioned, was the first successful Scots Colony in the New World administered solely by Scots.

In August of 1683, proprietor Samuel Groom, Surveyor General for Deputy-Governor Thomas Rudyard, wrote a letter to the Proprietors of East Jersey announcing that three of the proprietors' houses in Perth Amboy were completed and others ready to go up. houses were substantial structures for their time, each with a double chimney of wood and clay. The other proprietors directed Rudyard to reside in the town and establish courts. By 1684 Perth Amboy had been established as the seat of government for all East Jersey.

From his final confinement in prison Sir George Scott seems to have concluded that there was little to be gained by his resistance. Since whatever he had left would be lost by his continued defiance of an unjust law, the best solution was to emigrate. He seems to have proceeded about this in a businesslike way. From his prison cell he first addressed a petition to the Privy Council asking for his release to "go to the Plantations" and promised to take with him his wife's cousin, Archibald Riddle, considered to be one of the more obnoxious Covenanter preachers. He also offered to offer security of 5,000 merks to guarantee he would not return to Scotland. This petition was acted on April 1, 1684, and the Laird of Pitlochie found himself once more at liberty.

Using his political and social connections, Scott sought the support of the Proprietors of East Jersey. In 1685, to encourage his emigration scheme and attract other emigrants he spent several months compiling, printing, and circulating his book, *The Model of the Government of the Province of East Jersey, in America, and Encouragement for Such a Design to be concerned there.* In it he included a description written by Gawen Lawrie in which Lawrie described the condition of the East Jersey Colony:

> *There are a few stone houses but most are made of wood, the towns are not compactly built, but are straggling rural communities like many of those in New England—most of the towns are as in Maryland and Virginia, on the banks of streams where small vessels can land goods—wages are high; a workman can earn two shillings or half-a-crown a day and more...*

In the meantime the glowing description of colonial prosperity drawn by Lawrie and Scott was doing little to attract Scottish colonists. There was little interest in the prospect of being absorbed into a community of English farmers and tradesmen from Puritan New England who had already settled in New Jersey. Such emigration as there already was from Scotland was hardly the result of voluntary choice, but rather to secure political and religious freedom from oppression in Scotland. Sir George Scott was among those who took a leading role in extolling the virtues and attractiveness of East Jersey to his countrymen and the persecuted Covenanters.

Scott also arranged an additional land grant of 500 acres for himself from the Scots Proprietors, with the guarantee that he would improve and reside on it. Finally, he obtained the following agreement from the Earl of Perth to remove the persecuted Covenanters to America:

> *By the Right Honourable Earl of Perth, Lord High Chancellour of Scotland, These are permitting and allowing mr. George Scott of Pitlochie, with his lady, Children and Family, and such other Persons as he shall ingage, to pass from this Kingdom either by Sea or Land, to any of His Majestie's Forreigh Plantations providing such persons to be transported by him, be not Traitors, Rebels, Fugitives, and that without any Let, Impediment, or Molestation, from any person whatever: they always behaving themselves peaceably and according to the Law.*

## THE EARL OF PERTH

The presence of James Drummond, the Earl of Perth, among the proprietors, Royalist and high churchman though he was, was no obstacle to Scott's overall scheme. Perth's political and religious tenets were just a matter of convenience. Covenanters in Scotland were obnoxious to him for interfering with the system of government in which he had a personal interest. His inclusion, and that of others who may have thought as he did, was not likely to stand in the way of Scott's objectives. Thus it can be seen that the Proprietors of East Jersey included men of widely different views on politics and religion.

The Earl of Perth, Lord High Chancellor of Scotland

Sir George Scott successfully arranged to take many of the most uncompromising Presbyterian Covenanters from Scotland to Perth Amboy. Scott himself died on the long and arduous voyage, as did his wife, Lady Margaret, and her sister, Lady Atlhernie. Dr. John Johnstone and Sir George's daughter Eupham survived the voyage. They had fallen in love in Scotland. Dr. Johnstone was a scion of the noble House of Annandale and a member of the established Church of England. Eupham, like her parents, was a Presbyterian. Together during the crossing they attended their sick and dying fellow passengers. Eupham must have kept John guessing since they did not marry until 1686. Both remained closely identified with Perth Amboy and St. Peter's Church throughout their lives.

Dr. John Johnstone was destined to play a leading role in the history of New Jersey and New York City. As for the nonpaying passengers, upon arrival those who had promised to work as indentured servants for four years refused to abide by the terms of their financial agreement to redeem the cost of the expenses incurred by Scott for their transportation. This included the four years of indentured service now payable to Sir George's surviving heir, Eupham Scott. To compensate, according to *The Minutes of The Board of Proprietors of the Eastern Division of New Jersey from 1685 to 1705*, the following solution was recorded:

> *At a COUNCIL of the proprietors of the said province of East Jersey, held at Perth Amboy, the sixth day of June, Anno Dom. 1701*
>
> *Present Governor Hamilton, David Lyell, Miles Forster, John Johnstone, George Willocks, John Barclay, and Thomas Gordon, proprietors, proxies and Commissioners.*
>
> *Upon petition of John Johnstone, Esquire, for head land for himself and his wife (daughter of George of Pitlochie, deceased) for such people and servants as they imported into this province in the year 1685 upon the encouragement of the Proprietors in England, which comes to 3,050 acres, according to the list of names to the said petition annexed; agreed and ordered that he have it as desired in consideration of the great loss they did suffer as a result of importing the said people upon the proprietors' encouragement and which has contributed very much to the good of the province.*

To honor their memory, on May 4, 1929 a bronze tablet contributed by the Society of Colonial Wars in the State of New Jersey was erected in St. Peter's Church, Perth Amboy. Its inscription reads:

*To the Memory of*
*George Scott of Pitlochie, Margaret his wife, their daughter Eupham,*
*Doctor John Johnstone, and two hundred other exiles from Scotland,*
*who came from Leith to Perth Amboy in the ship "Henry and Francis,"*
*September-December, 1685.*

A second historic marker honoring the *Henry and Francis* was erected at the intersection of High and Lewis Streets for the 350th anniversary of Perth Amboy on November 23, 2008. It has now been placed in Caledonia Park on the cairn memorializing Perth Amboy's Scottish heritage. This marker not only honors the memory of the valiant passengers of the *Henry and Francis*, but also stands as a reminder to all who read its words of the many exiles who, because of religious or political persecution, were driven from their homelands to the United States of America.

It was anticipated by Sir George Scott that vast numbers of victims of the cruel religious and political persecutions raging in Scotland would seize the chance to emigrate to East Jersey. Between 1683 and 1685 perhaps 500 Scots of high and low estate arrived in Perth Amboy, most of whom settled in Middlesex, Somerset and Monmouth Counties. In time they came to exercise an influence that was out of proportion to their numbers. They were predominantly Presbyterians, and it was largely owing to their efforts that Presbyterianism became established in East Jersey and in the New World.

In 1688, the Roman Catholic King James II abdicated the throne during the English "Glorious Revolution," and Roman Catholic James Drummond, the Earl of Perth, fled to France. With the lessening threat of persecution and the death of Robert Barclay in 1690, organized Scottish emigration to Perth Amboy ceased.

## THE PRESBYTERIANS

After many years of meeting in private homes in Perth Amboy, between 1731 and 1735 the Presbyterian Covenanters established a meeting house adjacent to the site of the town's first seventeenth century "Burial Place" where their parents, wives, or children had been interred. This is the site of the old Perth Amboy High School on State Street. The present First Presbyterian Church on the southwest corner of Market and High Streets was built in 1902 where an earlier wooden frame church erected in 1802 had once stood.

The proprietors' initial motivating force was a desire to make East Jersey a haven for Scottish Quakers. Although their proposal for attracting Quakers was not as successful as it was in West Jersey, and the Scottish Proprietors' schemes for colonization lasted only a few short years, the settlement continued to attract new Scottish immigrants through the remainder of the eighteenth century. This established East Jersey as a key area of Scottish influence within the Middle Colonies, a fact emphasized during the struggles for political and economic independence that took place during the American Revolution.

It is a reasonable to assume that between 1763 and 1776 more than 50,000 people of Scottish blood from Scotland and Ulster [a province of Ireland], the so-called Scots-Irish, crossed the Atlantic to settle permanently in the American colonies. These vast emigrations were caused by economic depression and the proverty, misery and want brought on by famine. However the vast majority of passengers were Presbyterians seeking religious freedom and economic opportunity in America. They brought with them a typical Scottish system of values in honest toil and sturdy independence.

# PRESBYTERIANISM ESTABLISHED IN AMERICA

The first historian of the Province of East Jersey, Samuel Smith, described how early Scottish settlers settled principally in north and central New Jersey, which included the area around Perth Amboy. The Church Meeting House of Woodbridge that had been established by New England and Long Island Puritans (today called the Old White Church) accepted Archibald Riddle, the preacher, and seven fellow passengers from the *Henry and Francis* into its fold. Riddle in fact was minister of the church from 1686 to 1689.

Another twenty Covenanters from the *Henry and Francis* followed John Frazer, the strong leader of the Covenanters, to Bound Brook and joined the existing religious community there, founding the Church of Bound Brook in 1688. In 1692 other members of these political and religious dissenters found their way to Monmouth County and established a church on Free Hill in Wickatunk, Marlboro Township, known as Old Scots Meeting House.

# THE FIRST PRESBYTERY

Fourteen years later, on December 29, 1706, the Old Scots Meeting House became the seat of a presbytery, the very beginning of organized Presbyterianism in America. On May 29, 1706 the first Presbyterian minister in America, John Boyd, had been ordained at Old Scots. He died two years later, and his is the oldest grave in the adjacent burying ground. By January 17, 1707 Presbyterianism had been introduced in New York City, but not until 1722 was the First Presbyterian Church built there.

By 1730 the Old Scots Church became inadequate and the congregation decided to build a new Presbyterian church, Old Tennent Church, on White Hill in nearby Tennent, New Jersey. Founded by Scottish religious and political dissenters, it was used as a field hospital for wounded American soldiers as the Battle of Monmouth (June 28, 1778) raged around it.

The tombstones in Old Tennent's graveyard and in the fields beyond mark not only the final resting places of refugees from religious persecution in Scotland. They also denote the final resting places of blue-clad patriot Continentals and British redcoats, both lying side by side. This church regularly appears in leading surveys of American architecture and is a lasting shrine to freedom in the New World.

# THE RELIGIOUS SOCIETY OF FRIENDS (QUAKERS)

For administrative purposes, the Perth Amboy Quakers established a Monthly Meeting in that city in 1686. John Reid, the surveyor, was its clerk and George Keith, a recent arrival from Scotland, soon became a well-known member. Meeting privately in houses, they remained in Amboy until 1689. Afterwards they moved to Woodbridge, where a meeting had been organized in 1686 in the home of Benjamin Griffith.

By 1713 the Woodbridge Society of Friends had built a meeting house in that town. Later, since they refused to participate in patriot Revolutionary War activities, they were pressured to leave Woodbridge. Soon they moved to Rahway, after selling their Woodbridge meeting house to an early congregation of Methodists there. The Rahway meeting was eventually merged with the present Plainfield meeting, and Quakerism has remained a small sect in East Jersey to this day.

# THE ROYAL CAPITAL AT PERTH AMBOY

## NEW JERSEY AS A CROWN COLONY 1702-76

*"Man is in love and loves what vanishes; what more is there to say?"* -W. B. Yeats

The demography of the colonial and state capital of Perth Amboy (1683-1790) was much like that of other provincial cities. Three distinct social classes developed: first, an aristocracy based on wealth, made up of the great landowning proprietors; second, the independent farmers, skilled workers, small shopkeepers, and laborers; and third, the indentured servants and African slaves.

Here officers of the Crown mingled with local merchants who had grown rich while trading with the other North American colonies and the West Indies. Many of them lived in elegant houses staffed by numerous African slaves and attended the services of the Church of England at St. Peter's Church. Perth Amboy's status as the Scottish capital of East Jersey from 1686 to 1702, and afterward as one of New Jersey's twin royal capitals, made this city an important political and social center during the colonial period.

Philadelphia had nearly 25,000 people, and New York City had about 20,000 in 1765. In 1775, prior to the American Revolution, there were approximately three million residents in the colonies, but only one tenth lived in large towns or cities. By the end of the American Revolution the population of New Jersey was approximately 150,000 individuals, with slightly fewer than 10 percent being slaves or free blacks. According to William Whitehead, in 1759 Perth Amboy had about 100 houses. Another account in 1761 places the number closer to 200 structures. The statistics of the population, based on the Federal Census of 1810 as cited by historian William A. Whitehead, returned a population of 815; by 1830 there had been a slight increase to 879 inhabitants.

Although English and Dutch were the predominant languages in New Jersey, there were also French and German settlers from the Palatinate of the Rhine, and Scots and Scots-Irish, who were ethnically Scottish. While English was the common tongue in the area of New Jersey, many residents spoke the language with a distinct accent based on their countries of origin. The African-American population spoke the language of their masters, but vestiges of their own languages survived in expressions and idioms.

While leading patriots would soon be decrying the king's efforts to enslave his American subjects, African-American slavery was an accepted social institution in every American colony. Black slaves could be found working in shops in Boston or on the docks of New York City, in the elegant homes of Philadelphia's merchant elite, in the tobacco fields of Virginia, and in the rice paddies of South Carolina.

No matter where they lived, slaves endured hard and demeaning lives. On the whole, slaves were poorly fed and poorly clothed, and were often subjected to both physical and psychological abuse. From humiliating names to punishments, slaves learned the meaning of freedom every day by its absence in their lives.

## THE ISSUE OF SLAVERY

By 1737, New Jersey had one slave for every twelve people. In Perth Amboy, nearly every house "swarmed with African slaves performing domestic labor." It was in Perth Amboy where the Royal African Company established a major slave trading center, transporting shiploads of misery to America. Here thousands of imported African slaves were sold against their will. They arrived in the New World after being jammed below decks in dark holds, where they were typically shackled in pairs. Historians estimate that ten percent died during their Atlantic crossing and their bodies were subsequently heaved overboard.

As for discipline, it was at the whim of the owner, and the ultimate punishment of burning at the stake was not unheard of. At Perth Amboy, in 1729, an African man named Prince, charged with the murder of William Cook, was burned in this fashion. There were also public stocks on the southeast side of the Market Square to punish malefactors.

## AMONG THE ARISTOCRATS

The great mansions of Perth Amboy's eighteenth century aristocrats with whom Governor and Lady Franklin socialized—the Johnstones, Parkers, Skinners, and Kearnys—are long since demolished. Their homes were converted or destroyed by Tories, patriots, and the ravages of time. Even the Proprietary House could not escape a disastrous fire in 1786, which came close to leveling it.

From its origins, Perth Amboy was distinctively different from the other early communities of East Jersey. Despite its early pretensions to commercial greatness and not having realized the ambitions of its founders, Perth Amboy was a stronghold of Anglicanism. It was the residence of many of the influential proprietors and government officials, was one of the twin capitals of the province, a port of some consequence, the seat of culture and gentility, and a bastion of conservatism.

## THE JOHNSTONE FAMILY IN AMERICA

The Johnstones, in addition to the Parkers, Skinners, and Kearnys, all supported the last royal governor of New Jersey, William Franklin. As with the proprietors, the Johnstones' wealth and position in society was founded on their aristocratic heritage and great landholdings. The progenitor of the Johnstone Family in America was Dr. John Johnstone, a doctor of pharmacology. Through his wife Eupham Scott, daughter of Sir George Scott, they inherited all of Scott's proprietary land rights. When his brother James Johnstone of Spotswood died in 1697, John inherited all of his extensive land holdings. Together this amounted to thousands upon thousands of acres of land. Dr. Johnstone was a member of the King's Council in East Jersey from 1686 to 1688 and from 1704 to 1726.

As a member of the East Jersey Board of Proprietors, Dr. Johnstone was their signatory, surrendering the province to the Crown in 1702. His career of political service was remarkable in that he served with distinction in both the Province of East Jersey and the Province of New York at the same time. He was Mayor of the City of New York from 1714 to 1718, a member of the Governor's Council of the Province of New York from 1716 to 1722, and served on the Governor's Council of New Jersey under Governor William Burnet.

Johnstone was a member of the New York-New Jersey Boundary Commission of 1719-20, which settled the boundary of Staten Island. A member of the Provincial Assembly from Amboy between 1709 and 1710 and 1720 to 1732, he was Speaker of the Assembly for ten years. He sat in the Court of Common Right and he was also first in the list of men to whom Perth Amboy's charter from King George I was given. Always a devout Anglican, he served on the vestry of St. Peter's Church between the years 1722 and 1728 and 1730 to 1731. He died in 1732 and was interred in St. Peter's Churchyard. Johnstone Street in Perth Amboy was named in his honor. His wife, Eupham lived long enough to have known the last Royal Governor of New Jersey, William Franklin. She died in 1764.

# JOHN AND JAMES PARKER

The Parker Castle, whose stone section was constructed by Scottish stonemasons, and which had been home to eight generations of the illustrious Parker Family, was ignominiously torn down in the twentieth century to make way for an apartment complex. Until it was demolished in 1942, it was one of the oldest houses still standing in Perth Amboy. It served a dual purpose as a patriot lookout and as a barracks for British soldiers.

John Parker, who was responsible for building Perth Amboy's four-story stone-front "Parker Castle," was a descendant of Elisha Parker Sr., born in England in 1630. Elisha first settled first in Scituate, Massachusetts and later moved in Woodbridge, New Jersey in 1675. As a prosperous farmer, Elisha Parker Sr. sold some 60 of his Woodbridge acres in 1701 to his son Elisha Parker Jr., father of John Parker, who was born November 17, 1693. John Parker, who followed his father in the merchant business, was active in politics and was a prosperous merchant.

In 1722 John Parker was described as being "...one of his Majesties Council for the Province of New Jersey" when a man named John Campyon appeared before him in a case relating to a land transaction. John's son James would remain cautiously neutral during the Revolution. The Parker Castle served the officers of both patriot and British armies, which helps to explain why it was not confiscated or destroyed. John Parker's first cousin, James Parker of Woodbridge, who had met the distinguished printer William Bradford as early as 1723, became apprenticed to Bradford in 1726, and eventually brought the first permanent printing press to New Jersey. Parker Street is named for this family, who were prominent in Perth Amboy, the Colony, and the State of New Jersey for three centuries.

## WILLIAM BRADFORD AND GEORGE KEITH

William Bradford started teaching James Parker of Woodbridge his craft when Parker was just twelve years old. Before James's term of indenture had expired, he ran away to Philadelphia, where he met another printer, Benjamin Franklin, and established a lifelong friendship. James Parker owned and operated the first New Jersey print shop in Woodbridge. A replica of that print shop stands on Rahway Avenue (Route 514) just north of the Woodbridge Township town hall.

The English Quaker William Bradford, the first printer for the Quakers in the City of Philadelphia in 1688 and "...the pioneer printer of the Middle

Colonies," moved his business to New York City in 1693. He owned two lots in Perth Amboy and is thought to have built a house here in 1715.

As the official government printer to New Jersey from 1703 until 1733, Bradford was known to have printed documents for the provincial government in Perth Amboy on his portable printer (some think on the southeast corner of Smith and High Streets). But the first permanent print shop belonged to James Parker of Woodbridge.

It was in Philadelphia that Bradford met George Keith, a Scotsman who had been the superintendent of the Quaker schools in Philadelphia in 1689. Always in the storm of debate and skilled in argument, Keith battled with the Calvinism of Puritan New England and was a zealous defender of Quakerism.

Keith employed Bradford to print several pamphlets, including a 1691 defense of the Quakers against the Puritan attacks of Cotton Mather of Massachusetts. But then, dissatisfied with Quakers in America, Keith made Perth Amboy his headquarters for two years after he had been ordained in the Church of England, and had become its first general missionary in America.

The following references to Perth Amboy were published in Keith's *Journal of Travels* in 1706:

> *I preached at Amboy in East Jersey: the Auditory was small: My text Titus I: 11, 12. But such as were there were well affected. Some of them of my former Acquaintance and others who had been formerly Quakers but were come over to the church particularly Miles Forster and John Barclay (brother of Governor Robert Barclay). The place has very few inhabitants. We were several days kindly entertained by Miles Forster at his House there.*

Another reference from his *Journal of Travels* states: "On December 25, Christmas Day, 1703. I preached at Amboy, at my Lord Cornbury's lodging where he was present and many with him. My text was John 12: 35 and 36."

# PROPRIETORS SURRENDER TO THE CROWN

Many questions continued to be raised in the seventeenth century about the legality of the proprietors' right to govern. These were resolved on April 15, 1702 when Dr. John Johnstone signed the documentation in Perth Amboy for the East Jersey Board of Proprietors ceding the proprietors' governing powers to the Crown and Anne, Queen of both Scotland and England. Two days later New Jersey formally became a Royal Colony. However, the proprietors retained their rights to all lands they owned under the original royal grant or for which no clear title existed, and continued to be prominent in New Jersey government, receiving important appointments from the Crown.

The two Jerseys (East and West) were now united to form a single royal province under one Royal Governor, and so began a new era in the political history of New Jersey. The governmental authority had passed from the self-serving hands of the proprietors to a ponderous bureaucracy in England, assisted by royal appointees and royal governors—all officers of the Crown. The government was now conducted alternately at the twin capitals of Perth Amboy and Burlington, and many guarantees were bestowed on the proprietors to give them a preferred political position in the province. St. Peter's Church in Perth Amboy holds treasured remembrance of this period—five pieces of hand-wrought communion silver given to the church by Queen Anne, probably about 1706, a rare and exceptional collection. The chalice is marked "Annae Reginae," and was crafted by William Gibson, Corey Lane, London, who registered his maker's mark in April 1697.

After the War for Independence, the State of New Jersey adopted a policy of recognizing land titles from any longtime occupant of the land. The proprietors' prerogative survived the Revolution unimpeded. Operating out of their last Surveyor General's Office in Perth Amboy from 1852 until 1998, the contemporary proprietors of East Jersey realized that they had no more land to sell and voted themselves out of business. Their extensive archives were donated to the New Jersey State Library. Their vacated office, adjacent to City Hall, was given to the City of Perth Amboy to be utilized for historic purposes, allowing visitors to linger over the amazing physical evidence of centuries past.

The act for the union of two kingdoms of England and Scotland was passed in the summer of 1709 in which both England and Scotland were united into one kingdom to be called Great Britain. During this Royal period in New Jersey few changes were as significant as the one to do with the governor. Until 1738, New Jersey shared its governor with New York. Royal appointees tended to devote the greater part of their time to the affairs of New York, the result of which was that New Jersey suffered from their neglect.

# THE ROYAL GOVERNORS

## RESIDENT GOVERNOR LORD CORNBURY

In 1701 King William and Queen Mary named Edward, Lord Viscount Cornbury, Governor of New York. He was a grandson of the great Lord Chancellor under Charles II who was Henry Hyde, the second Earl of Clarendon. In 1702, Mary's sister, Queen Anne, gave Cornbury the governorship of the newly created Crown Colony in New Jersey.

Lord Cornbury, who was a cousin of Queen Anne, first arrived in New Jersey in the summer of 1703. In November 1703 he called his first Provincial Assembly in Perth Amboy demanding that his personal revenue be increased in order to recoup his lost fortune from his libertine, incompetent lifestyle.

He remained in Amboy at Edinborough Castle, the governor's residence, through Christmas 1703. He served through a highly controversial period with the resident Scots Proprietors until 1708. Edinborough Castle, the foundations of which still survive, may have been built for Andrew Hamilton, resident Deputy Governor of East Jersey from March 1687 to August 1688 and Governor of both East and West Jersey from April 1692 to April 1698.

# RESIDENT ROYAL GOVERNOR ROBERT HUNTER

Following Lord Cornbury there were two interim governors from 1708 to 1710—John Lovelace, Baron of Hurley, and Richard Ingoldesby. They were followed in turn by Robert Hunter, Governor from 1710 until 1720. Born in Edinburgh, Hunter was the grandson of the Laird of Hunterston. Through a corruption of Hunterston, his former home in Scotland, Hunterdon County, New Jersey was named for him in 1714. As a resident governor, he owned extensive New Jersey property, including more than one house in Perth Amboy and 500 acres bordering the shores of the Raritan River.

Built in 1710, Governor Hunter's Perth Amboy residence was at 129 Water Street. Hunter would often retire here to obtain rest from the heavy burdens of his administration of both New Jersey and New York. Hunter's home later became "Pleasant View," and was the home of Commodore Thomas Truxton, who entertained Vice-President Aaron Burr here after his fatal duel with Alexander Hamilton on July 11, 1804. Thomas Jefferson subsequently dropped Aaron Burr from his reelection ticket of 1804, choosing Governor George Clinton of New York instead. Later Commodore Jacob Lewis was to live at "Pleasant View." Lewis Street is named in his honor.

As the king's representative, Robert Hunter presented the Royal Charter, granted by King George I, to St. Peter's Church on July 30, 1718 and a Royal Charter to the City of Perth Amboy on August 24, 1718. While the city was incorporated under both proprietary and royal governments, its present charter, embracing the provisions of the prior ones, was granted in 1784.

# RESIDENT ROYAL GOVERNOR WILLIAM BURNET

William Burnet governed from 1720 until 1728 and purchased Governor Hunter's residence on Water Street for his use while in Perth Amboy. Although governor of both New Jersey and New York, he spent the vast majority of his time in New York City. He subsequently became Governor of Massachusetts and New Hampshire and died on September 7, 1729 from the lingering injuries suffered in a carriage accident in Boston. According to W. Northley Jones, when Burnet died he was buried "...in an ancient graveyard just north of the Westminster (Proprietary House) on Kearny Avenue."

In digging the foundations for a house (about 1909) the gravestone of one Benjamin Harrison was uncovered and removed to St. Peter's Churchyard. The location of the *ancient graveyard* has not since been determined. According to Governor Burnet's will, he wished to be buried next to his second wife Mary Van Horn at the chapel at Fort James, located at the Battery of New York City. This fort was destroyed in 1790.

Two governors whose terms were shortened by their deaths succeeded William Burnet—John Montgomerie of Dumfriesshire, Scotland, who governed from 1728 to 1731, who died of smallpox then raging in New York, and William Cosby, who governed from 1732 to 1736, and died of tuberculosis in New York City.

## ROYAL GOVERNOR LEWIS MORRIS

Lewis Morris governed from 1738 through 1746, and was one of New Jersey's most influential leaders. Morris had previously served as President of the East Jersey Board of Proprietors from 1725 until 1730. He was a fierce adherent and defender of Royal authority.

Morris's father moved from Barbados to today's Bronx, New York, where he purchased 3,000 acres and established an estate which he called Morrisania. Lewis was born there in 1691 and thus was the first American-born Royal Governor of New Jersey. He not only inherited this estate but also one at Tintern, now called Tinton Falls, in Monmouth County, New Jersey. His inherited wealth placed him among the elites of New York and New Jersey. His labor force of some 66 slaves made him one of the largest slaveholder in the Middle Colonies.

For thirty-five years Lewis Morris's main preoccupation was politics, and he held many important offices in both New York and New Jersey. Morris County and Morristown, New Jersey are named in his honor. Lewis Morris was the grandfather of the Lewis Morris who signed the Declaration of Independence for the state of New York.

## ROYAL GOVERNOR JONATHAN BELCHER

Governor Jonathan Belcher, who governed from 1747 to 1757 was born in Cambridge, Massachusetts into a family that was rooted in New England Puritan society. He landed in Perth Amboy on August 8, 1747, having come by barge from Sandy Hook. The voyage across the Atlantic was made on the man-of-war HMS *Scarborough*. He made Elizabethtown his New Jersey residence and his private residence, one of New Jersey's best-preserved architectural gems, still stands on Jersey Avenue in Elizabeth. He frequently called the Assembly to meet in Elizabeth, avoiding the tradition of alternating meetings between Perth Amboy and Burlington.

## RESIDENT ROYAL GOVERNOR SIR FRANCIS BERNARD

Sir Francis Bernard, born in Brightwell, Oxfordshire, England, was Royal Governor of New Jersey for two years (from 1758 until 1760). Bernardsville, New Jersey is named in his honor. After being knighted in 1769, he landed at Perth Amboy on June 14, 1758, stepping down from his majesty's ship *The Terrible* with his wife and family. The second day after his arrival he met with members of his council and the Mayor of Perth Amboy, Samuel Neville, Esq., and proceeded to the old Court House (the City Hall), New Jersey's colonial and state capitol building on Market Square. Here, as was the tradition, he mounted the steps and read his commission aloud. A few days later he traveled to Burlington to do the same.

Historian William A. Whitehead tells us that while in New Jersey, Francis Bernard's residence was in the old Johnstone mansion at Amboy, which stood about halfway between the Long Ferry and Sandy Point. The Bell family mansion replaced it in 1795, which was situated at 105 Kearny Avenue well into the 1930s. Both structures have long since disappeared. However, there is reason to believe that the Governor's House was still standing and that Governor Francis Bernard made his residence there. After a short administration he departed Perth Amboy on a warship bound for Boston after King George II had appointed him governor of Massachusetts.

## ROYAL GOVERNORS BOONE AND HARDY

Governors Thomas Boone, who governed between 1760 and 1761, was born in Kent, England. Josiah Hardy, who succeeded him as governor from 1761 until 1763, was also born in England. Both were weak appointees. Boone, although well liked, left his governorship to accept a more appealing appointment by the king as Royal Governor of South Carolina. Hardy was recalled from office because of a flagrant violation of his instructions with regard to the manner of appointing justices. This opening would be filled by the royal appointment of William Franklin.

# HISTORIC BUILDINGS AND PERSONAGES

## JOHN WATSON

Known as the first portrait painter to settle in America, John Watson, born in Scotland in 1685, immigrated to Perth Amboy in 1714. His remains lie interred in St. Peter's Churchyard. Watson had the first art studio and gallery in America, located on the southwest corner of Water and Market Streets. Here he both painted and sold his and other artists' works of art.

Watson painted many prominent New Jersey figures, among them Royal Governor William Burnet (in about 1720), and William Eier, Mayor of Perth Amboy from 1721 to 1723. Both of these portraits are currently owned by the New Jersey Historical Society. Watson also painted New Jersey Royal Governor Lewis Morris, and this portrait is owned by the Brooklyn Museum. The Pennsylvania Historical Society owns Watson's miniatures of Governor William Keith and his wife. Watson Avenue is named in his honor.

John Watson's art studio no longer exists and the great days of Perth Amboy's role as a seaport are long over. The waterside streets that had once thronged with ships in wharves have all passed into history. Gone are the famous inns, the Long Ferry and King's Arms taverns, long-absent gathering places where the old salts—fishermen and pilots—gathered to tell their avid audiences numerous tales, each no doubt better than the last.

## THE KING'S ARMS

The public house (from which the word "pub" derives) during British rule was called the King's Arms, or The Hicks Tavern. Whitehead names Hicks as its innkeeper since it was called The Hicks tavern during the American Revolution. It stood on the northwest corner of High and Smith Streets. At the peak of its popularity during the Revolution, it counted among its many guests colonial public officials and prominent Revolutionary War figures alike. George and Martha Washington stayed here on May 22, 1776, and in March of 1780 Alexander Hamilton more likely than not also stayed here. Here guests met, dined, and rested from their travels. It was also a well-known setting to take in the news from the outside world. Often plainspoken talk of civil war turned its smoky taproom gray.

Taverns or inns were an absolute necessity during colonial times. In fact, a 1668 law ordered every East Jersey town to provide an "ordinary" for the relief and entertainment of strangers. The local "ordinary" was a social and political center of unrivaled importance. The taproom was constantly enlivened by the presence of local gentry and frivolity.

The tavern also served as a social center where local news was exchanged and revolution was fomented. Visitors and townspeople all gathered in a main assembly room in front of a wide fireplace. After drinks were dispensed and food served, guests raised their voices in a roaring song or perhaps in a heated argument. Sleeping rooms were commonly situated above the taproom, and guests often slept two or more to a bed.

A 1704 New Jersey law sentenced four hours in the public stocks for public drunkenness, and forbade anyone to drink on the Lord's Day, a stricture considerably watered down by the clause "excepting for necessary refreshments." The public stocks at Perth Amboy stood in the Market Square, a few feet south of the old market house itself.

The act "...for building barracks within the colony..." provided that any tavern keeper who sold liquor to common soldiers without permission of their commanding officers or from a justice of the peace should forfeit forty shillings.

A law passed by the New Jersey Provincial Assembly in 1778 made it the duty of the court to ascertain, before issuing any license, whether the tavern keeper applicant possessed sufficient means to enable him to provide a certain number of featherbeds for the use of travelers, as well as stabling and pasturage for horses.

## THE BRITISH BARRACKS

In 1758 the great Perth Amboy British Barracks were erected just west of old North Dock Street (present-day Commerce Street). It was the largest by far of the five British barracks built in New Jersey, built between 1758 and 1759. Erected by the British for their troops during the French and Indian War, other barracks were located in Burlington, Trenton, New Brunswick, and Elizabeth. The one at Perth Amboy was much larger than even the Boston city jail, and it was first occupied by troops returning from the Siege of Havana in 1761. Afterwards a regiment of British troops was usually stationed there. They stood at the head of Barracks Street, and were demolished in 1909.

While the Trenton barracks is the only one that has survived to this day, there is a replica of the New Brunswick barracks at East Jersey Olde Town Village in Piscataway, just over the Raritan River from New Brunswick.

The British Barracks

# THE LONG FERRY AND TAVERN

In addition to the King's Arms, colonial Perth Amboy had another well-known tavern. The Long Ferry Tavern was one of four stone buildings built by the proprietors in 1685 on the so called "Long Ferry" property at the foot of High Street, the present site of Caledonia Park. The name "Caledonia" is the ancient name of Scotland. And before Edinburgh, the ancient capital of Scotland was named Perth.

From the foot of High Street this ferry would ply back and forth to South Amboy where it met Lawrie's Road that led to Burlington, the capital of West Jersey. This property was given the name "Long Ferry" to distinguish it from the other ferry—the shorter one that ran between Perth Amboy and Tottenville, Staten Island from the Town Wharf at the foot of Dock Street (present-day Fayette Street).

In his autobiography Benjamin Franklin describes how in 1719, as he traveled from Boston to New York to seek his fortune, he passed through Perth Amboy. Franklin took the ferry at Billop's Landing on Staten Island to the Town Wharf. From there he walked down High Street to the Long Ferry Tavern and arranged to board the Long Ferry to South Amboy. Then, during a two-day journey on foot, Franklin walked across New Jersey to Burlington on Lawrie's Road.

As a boy of seventeen Benjamin Franklin had no idea he would make several return visits here as the father of a future Royal Governor of New Jersey and on September 11, 1776 as an American Peace Commissioner.

# THE CHURCH OF ENGLAND

## ST. PETER'S CHURCH–THE STATE CHURCH

Meeting in private homes at first, the Anglicans of Perth Amboy used one of the four stone houses on the Long Ferry property in 1685 as the earliest public meeting place for their members. When the east end of the chancel extension of St. Peter's Church was constructed in 1905, a stone bearing the date 1685 , suggesting that it came from one of the first four stone houses of Perth Amboy, was inserted into the rear wall of the church, where it can still be seen today.

Historian William S. Pavlovsky disputes this fact. In his *Old Perth Amboy Walking Guide* Pavlovsky states that the stone bearing the date 1685 "...was more likely salvaged along with other materials from the ruins of David Mundie's 'Great Stone House,' which occupied this site from 1685 until its destruction, probably by fire sometime before 1718." One of the Long Ferry stone houses built in 1685 was used as a courthouse in 1695 and later in 1698 was transformed into the first St. Peter's Church building. St. Peter's predates Trinity Church, Wall Street, New York City.

In about 1695 several East Jersey proprietors applied to the Bishop of London for the appointment of an Anglican clergyman. At that time the majority of the early settlers were members of the Church of England, including those of Scottish ancestry. Consequently, in 1698, the Rev. Edward Portlock was sent to Perth Amboy and became the first Anglican clergyman of New Jersey and of St. Peter's Church.

The first permanent Perth Amboy Anglican Church building was built in 1719. On this site once stood David Mundie's horse-powered gristmill, which was used to provide flour for the settlement. One of the millstones that was used to grind the flour can still be viewed in the churchyard. Near this millstone is a bell presented to this parish by a Scottish-born sea captain from the Bahamas. It bears the inscription: "In Perth Amboy My Sound Enjoy–1789."

To show how closely St. Peter's Church was identified with the city and how the leading citizens in government were also members of St. Peter's, here is a listing of the offices that they held under the church charter as well as the city charter:

William Eier was the Senior Warden of the Church and

Mayor of the City

John Barclay was the Junior Warden and the City Clerk

Thomas Gordon was Vestryman and Secretary of the Province

John Rudyard was Vestryman and Alderman

Robert King, afterward Warden, was a charter citizen

John Stevens, Vestryman and deputy to conventions, was Chamberlain and Treasurer of the City

George Willocks was a charter member of both the church and city

Dr. John Johnstone, afterward a Vestryman, was a charter citizen

John Hamilton, afterward a Vestryman and Warden,

was a charter citizen

John Sharp, afterward a Vestryman, was a charter citizen

James Alexander, afterward a Vestryman, was recorder of the City

The present church was constructed in 1852. This church's beautiful interior contains a series of English-made historical stained glass windows with unique colonial themes. Some of them include the giving of the Communion

St Peter's Church and Churchyard

silver to St. Peter's Church by Queen Anne in 1706, the presentation of the church's charter from King George I in 1718, and the historic Peace Conference held in nearby Staten Island on September 11, 1776.

Interred in the churchyard among many early settlers and prominent citizens of Perth Amboy are Dr. Robert McKean, Rector of St. Peter's Church and founder of the New Jersey Medical Society (the oldest such society in the United States), and Samuel Neville, editor of the first successful magazine published in America, *The New American Magazine* (1760-1770), which chronicled the French and Indian War, among many other topics. Samuel Neville's family was from Strafford, England. For several years before coming to America Neville was editor of *The London Morning Post.*

## SAMUEL NEVILLE

Neville settled in Perth Amboy in May of 1736 to assume the proprietary interests he had inherited from his deceased sister, who had in turn inherited them from her husband. He served in the New Jersey Provincial Assembly and as Speaker of the House. He also served for 16 years as a judge on the New Jersey Provincial Supreme Court. Neville Street is named in his honor. After coming to Perth Amboy, Neville found it a pleasant town. The majority of the houses in the historic district were two stories high along the major town streets. Most homes had a garden, a well, and a cellar, and while some were made of stone, others were constructed of wood. Colonial Perth Amboy trades included blacksmiths hammering at anvils, wheelwrights, gunsmiths, harness makers, tailors, weavers, stonemasons and bricklayers, toolmakers and carpenters, among others.

Perth Amboy would have been a busy place at this time, with horses and carriages crowding the streets, pigs and chickens in pens clucking and crowing in private yards, and cattle and sheep in nearby pastures. There were local merchants lining the main streets, and a port filled with tall ships from the West Indies and other American colonies. American merchants and sailors were a constant presence in the British Caribbean. (There were twenty-six, not thirteen, colonies in British North America including the Caribbean Islands.)

Neville marveled at how the broad meandering of the Raritan River flowed into Raritan Bay at Perth Amboy and how a peaceful city surrounded a town marketplace square intersected by High Street. This street was used as parade grounds alternately for the British troops and then the patriots' Flying Camp, Washington's militia brigades stationed in this city during the summer and fall of 1776. In the center of the market square was the Market House where produce and livestock were sold, and thousands of slaves were imported into the colony in misery by the Royal African Company.

To the southeast of the square was St. Peter's Church with its tall steeple and nearby the Proprietors' Provincial Record Office (now at 53-55 Gordon Street). Originally one story high with a hip roof, this important colonial building was later converted and still stands as a private residence.

On the southwest corner of the Market Square and High Street was the Thomas Bartow House, Perth Amboy's second oldest residence, circa 1730, now moved back to 83-85 Market Street. William Dunlap, the playwright and art historian, received informal instruction in art and literature from the elderly Bartow during boyhood visits here. It was later the residence of the Smith family, after whom Smith Street is named. Thomas Bartow's niece, Theodosia Prevost, who married Vice President Aaron Burr Jr., was the daughter of his brother, Theodosius Bartow.
In his *History of the American Theatre*, Dunlap wrote,

> *I knew of Thomas Bartow, Samuel Neville and John Smyth, the three officials charged with seeing to the construction and furnishing the Perth Amboy Barracks. Mr. Bartow is known to be a small thin old man, with straight gray hair, pale face, plain dark–colored clothes, and stockings to suit–his well polished square-toed shoes, ornamented with little silver buckles.... When he walked, a cane with an ivory head aided his steps, which halted through age and rheumatism.... His house stood at the corner of the Market Square; it was surrounded on three sides by a garden with the best fruits our climate affords.*

After Thomas Barstow's death his son Thomas, a resident of Philadelphia, sold the property to James Hude Kearny. His daughter, Gertrude Parker Kearny married Charles McKnight Smith, M.D., the grandson of William Smith, the first Yale graduate to practice law in America. The great-great grandson of Dr. Smith, Charles K. Paul, II is a member of St. Peter's Church and a lifelong friend and distant cousin of the author through Elias Parker Sr., who settled in Woodbridge in 1675.

Perth Amboy City Hall

# THE OLD COURTHOUSE

On the northeast corner of Market Square stood the City Hall or Courthouse, built circa 1714, which contained the town jail. It still stands as part of the present City Hall, and the colonial jail is in its basement. Now the oldest municipal building in continuous use in the United States, it predates the city's incorporation. Having been originally erected as the second Middlesex County Courthouse, it continued to serve until the county seat was moved to New Brunswick in 1793. It is one of the most precious architectural possessions of colonial Perth Amboy and one of only a handful of eighteenth century high-style architectural building examples remaining in Middlesex County.

Prior to 1790 the courthouse served as New Jersey's colonial and state capitol, since the legislature met here and in Burlington, the West Jersey Capital, in alternate years. Considering how "birth pangs of freedom and equality" were acted out in the city of Perth Amboy, it was altogether fitting that it was here on November 20, 1789, that New Jersey became the first state to ratify the Bill of Rights. The present city of Trenton was selected as the new capital in 1790.

Freedom and equality were the premise and promise of the American Revolution, but legal freedom and political equality were denied African-Americans from the beginning of the republic. Given the great odds they had to contend with, and even with the knowledge that those words didn't apply to them, their human spirit remained strong.

The date March 31, 1870 is very significant in our national history. For this is the day when Thomas Mundy Peterson cast his vote in a municipal referendum at old Courthouse, the day following the adoption of the Fifteenth Amendment to the U.S. Constitution allowing all adult males regardless of color to vote. This made him the first African-American voter in the United States. A member of St. Peter's Church, Peterson is interred in its churchyard.

# ROYAL GOVERNOR WILLIAM FRANKLIN

## 1774-76

*"There is no greater weakness than stubbornness. If you cannot yield, if you cannot learn that there must be compromise in life—you lose."* -Maxwell Maltz

Between 1762-64 the proprietors of East Jersey had built the great Proprietary House, a showcase of wealth and power to serve as the official residence for the Royal Governor, William Franklin. John Edward Prior, the celebrated Scottish architect and master builder of London, designed the palatial manor house and supervised its construction. Prior, who had arrived in New York City in 1761, also conducted work for William Alexander (also known as Lord Stirling) on his homes in New York City and Basking Ridge, New Jersey.

William Alexander had been president of the East Jersey Board of Proprietors, and had attended their meetings in Perth Amboy. Alexander would totally disregard William Franklin's reminders of Alexander's frequent statement at Franklin's council table in Burlington that "a man ought to be dammed who would take up arms against his sovereign." During the Revolution Major General William Alexander would command a brigade at the Battle of Long Island and also serve at the battles of Trenton, Brandywine, Germantown, and Monmouth while William Franklin was incarcerated in a Connecticut jail.

The Proprietary House

# THE ROYAL GOVERNOR'S PALACE

Perth Amboy's pre-eminent high-style historic landmark, the Proprietary House, intended to be the royal governor's palace, was built on four levels (basement, two stories and an attic), with four chimneys and a hip roof pierced by dormers. At the time of its completion it was one of the largest and most elegant mansions in the thirteen American colonies.

The monumental severity of the original English Georgian structure is reflected in the high sandstone basement, belt and stringcourses, and heavy keystone lintels over the windows. The original property consisted of eleven acres and fronted on High Street until the early twentieth century when present day Kearny Avenue was cut through the original estate.

The proprietors of East Jersey sought to enhance their political power by having the royal governor, William Franklin, reside in Perth Amboy.

But it wasn't until after William Franklin had had a series of personal financial reverses and had ordered elaborate remodeling—a new-framed coach house, stables, fencing, painting, and wallpapering had been completed—that the sole, illegitimate son of Benjamin Franklin took up residence in October of 1774. Here he would be among likeminded British sympathizers.

Still standing on a rise overlooking Raritan Bay, the Proprietary House at 149 Kearny Avenue is the only official royal governor's residence of which any original part still remains in the thirteen colonies.

## ROYAL GOVERNOR WILLIAM FRANKLIN

Together with his wife, Lady Elizabeth (Downes) Franklin, William Franklin resided at the Proprietary House between October 1774 and June 1776. As relations between the Crown and the colonies deteriorated, so did relations between the royal governor and his famous father, Benjamin Franklin.

William Franklin's loyalty to King George III caused a tragic rift with his well-known patriot father. While Benjamin chose to reject his mother country, his son chose to disobey his father. The elder Franklin never forgave his estranged son for his disloyalty, and the Franklins illustrate the personal tragedy of families rent by the American Revolution.

As William Franklin strolled on Perth Amboy's bluff to enjoy the fresh air and view of Raritan Bay after his arrival in the fall of 1774, the ships in Perth Amboy's port were constant reminders of his boyhood home in Philadelphia.

As a child, during long periods of boredom when not kite flying in spring, swimming and fishing in summer, or skating and sledding in the long winter months, William would become restless as he watched ships arriving with goods from as far away as India. It would be only a matter of time before William, at age fifteen, would do as his father had done and try to run away to sea.

Instead, at the age of twenty-one, William joined a regiment of Pennsylvania troops and fought in the French and Indian War at Saratoga and Albany. Returning to Philadelphia with a rank of Captain of the Grenadiers, he had missed his father's initial experiments with electricity. But when Benjamin was ready to experiment with drawing lightning from the sky with the aid of a kite and a key, it was William who designed the kite and raced across a cow pasture in an electrical storm to get the kite aloft while Benjamin stood under the shelter of a shed.

Musing as he looked out over the bay from Perth Amboy's bluff, William could recall how he had yearned to go to London and how his father had paid his expenses to study law at the Middle Temple, assuring him that he would become a leading American lawyer. William had crammed massive doses of law and by the autumn term of 1758 was ready to stand before the Masters of the Bench at Middle Temple for a grueling oral examination, a prerequisite to being admitted to the English bar.

When Benjamin Franklin received an honorary doctorate degree from Oxford in 1762, William received an honorary master's degree from Oxford. To be a member of the elite was to be educated in Britain. William had become an English gentleman.

George Washington, by contrast, had never set foot in England, or indeed any part of Europe. His total schooling hardly went beyond what we would consider the elementary grades. His father died when he was eleven, carrying away with him any hope of receiving an education abroad. The only ocean trip Washington ever made was to accompany his half-brother Lawrence to Barbados, in hopes that a tropical climate would help Lawrence to recover from violent tuberculosis.

William remembered attending a London party and meeting Elizabeth Downes, daughter of a wealthy Barbados sugar planter. By the spring of 1761, as King George III waited to be crowned, William and Elizabeth became fixtures of London society, dancing at balls, strolling in Saint James's Park, and frequently attending the theatre at Covent Garden.

So high was William's rising star that he was invited to the coronation of George III. William marched in the royal procession into Westminster Abbey, to an assigned seat, while Benjamin Franklin had to stand outside. As

His Royal Majesty King George III was about to leave Westminster Abbey, a large jewel fell from his crown, an omen that was remembered in later years, when Great Britain lost the American colonies. The jewel was immediately recovered, but the colonies were not.

Soon thereafter the new Prime Minister, the Earl of Bute, informed the Board of Trade that the king "...was pleased to appoint William Franklin, Esq. to be Governor of Nova Caesarea, or New Jersey." For the rest of William's life this was to be his glory—that he was the first royal governor appointed by the new king.

William would always remember that day when at the age of thirty-two, and married less than one week, he was ushered into the presence of the young king and Lord Bute at St. James's Palace. After bending his right knee, he took the king's hands into his own white-gloved hands and kissed them, then rose to receive his commission and recite his oath of office. But at this hour of his son's greatest triumph, Benjamin Franklin left England alone, having skipped his own son's marriage ceremony.

William Franklin could recollect the icy bitter-cold morning of February 25, 1763 when as an elegant young governor, he shrugged off his bearskin coat and mounted the steps of the old courthouse in Perth Amboy before a shivering crowd to recite his commission, his first official act before a crowd of loyal subjects. In his mercifully short remarks following this recitation, William Franklin showed himself a true politician.

"I thank you for your kind congratulations" he told the city's residents. "The esteem which you so gratefully and justly express for my predecessors is no less agreeable to me. And wherever I may reside, which is as yet uncertain, I shall be glad of every opportunity of showing my regard for the city of Perth Amboy." He then led the way down High Street where toasts and a celebration followed at the nearby King's Arms Tavern.

Although the East Jersey Board of Proprietors had had the Proprietary House constructed as the royal governor's residence, Franklin had decided to reside on his plantation, "Strawberry Hill" in Rancocas, not far from Burlington, the West Jersey capital.

# THE FRENCH AND INDIAN WAR

The new governor of 70,000-odd farmers and townspeople had his job cut out for him. As a result of signing the Treaty of Paris in 1763, New Jersey, the second smallest populace of the American colonies, next to Delaware, owed a debt of £300,000, the highest in America, largely caused by the extensive system of its British barracks. Because the colonists had profited from various Crown expenditures, including bankrolling and winning the French and Indian War, Parliament decided that they should be subjected to taxation.

The colonists responded that since they were not represented in Parliament they should not be taxed by that body. To pay this debt the British Parliament issued the hated Stamp Act of November 1, 1765. Although the Stamp Act imposed a greater fiscal burden on the Caribbean West Indies than on North America, Jamaica and Barbados paid stamp duties, in contrast to the thirteen mainland colonies.

The period of the Seven Years' War, or, as it is otherwise known, the French and Indian War, from 1754 to 1763, was a time of change in North America. It remade America. In the end France transferred Canada and all French territory to the east of the Mississippi River, excepting French Louisiana, to Great Britain.

This period also saw the first artistic celebrations of the scenic wonders in America. Among these were impressive landscapes, mountains, river valleys, lakes, and waterfalls. Reflecting his opulent tastes, William Franklin would later request that the East Jersey Board of Proprietors have wallpaper with scenes of the falls of the Niagara and the Passaic Rivers hung in the grand entrance hall of the Proprietary House.

# THE STAMP ACT

James Parker of Woodbridge was among those who denounced the stamp tax in his letter to Attorney General Cortlandt Skinner of Perth Amboy, soon to become Governor Franklin's closest ally. All over New Jersey there were protests. When the stamps arrived off New York on the HMS *Royal Charlotte*, Governor Franklin refused to let them be landed in Perth Amboy or New Jersey. Later after the repeal of the Stamp Act on March 17, 1766 and during the Townshend Acts, dated June 29, 1767, Franklin openly refused to support the hated customs service and acted with great tact and discretion where conflict between Royal authority and local interests were threatened.

In September of 1774 the First Continental Congress assembled at Philadelphia to protest the British closing of the Port of Boston after the Tea Party nine months earlier. As the Sons of Liberty formed in 1765 in protest to the Stamp Act, protest and stirring up of patriot sympathy strengthened non-importation of tea in New Jersey. Governor Franklin gravely addressed the Provincial Assembly in Perth Amboy, just four months before the Battles of Lexington and Concord and what Henry Wadsworth Longfellow would refer to as "the shot heard 'round the world." Said William Franklin:

> *It is not for me to decide on the particular merits of the dispute between Great Britain and her colonies. Nor do I mean to censure those who conceive themselves aggrieved for aiming at a redress of the grievances. It is a duty they owe themselves, their country, and their posterity. All that I could wish to guard you against is the giving of any countenance or encouragement to that destructive mode of proceeding.... You have now pointed out to you, gentlemen, two roads, one evidently leading to peace, happiness, and a restoration of the public tranquility—the other inevitably conducting you to anarchy, misery, and all the horrors of a civil war.*

## CHARTERING QUEEN'S COLLEGE

Although Franklin's term of office began just as the colonial crisis of the mid-eighteenth century was coming to a head, William Franklin was one of the most popular and successful of all of the royal governors of New Jersey. He effectively represented the Crown and the people of New Jersey from 1763 to 1776.

Franklin's judgments on Indian policy, creating the Lenape reservation at Indian Mills in Burlington County, and his support for internal improvements and legal reforms, including the chartering of Rutgers University (then Queen's College) in 1766 were well-received in New Jersey. Franklin also pushed vigorously for badly-needed reforms. Among them was his campaign for better roads and bridges built with the proceeds of public lotteries.

## TREASURY STOLEN

After a decade of push and tug, Governor Franklin and the Provincial Assembly parted company in 1773 in a dispute over the theft of East Jersey tax receipts from a trunk in the Perth Amboy home of Treasurer Stephen Skinner. Skinner was a member of the so-called "Perth Amboy Group," a close-knit coterie of wealthy landowning East Jersey Proprietors, mercantile magnates, and lawyers of considerable political influence.

The loss of this substantial sum was a severe strain on an economy already plagued by a shortage of liquid capital, shrinking credit, and general deflation. Although Franklin had the thieves hunted down, the Assembly insisted that the wealthy Perth Amboy aristocrat had been negligent and demanded Skinner's resignation and additional restitution.

This matter strained the governor's political influence and prestige. Skinner, loyal to the royal cause, fled New Jersey in March 1776 and emigrated to Nova Scotia in 1777. Afterward, the properties of hundreds of Loyalists were confiscated and sold under legislation enacted in 1777. When the war ended, thousands of erstwhile Jerseymen and their families went into a harsh exile in Nova Scotia rather than endure the taunts of their old neighbors.

# THE RESIDENCE OF THE ROYAL GOVERNOR

# THE PROPRIETARY HOUSE

## *A Royal Palace*

Angered with his father's politics, Governor Franklin took a bold step when he made his decision to move the seat of government from his home near Burlington to the Proprietary House in Amboy in October 1774. Here he could be near his close friends on the council as he confronted a growing crisis. Lady Franklin welcomed the move to elegant Perth Amboy, since the city boasted a cosmopolitan mixture of music, bright talk, and intelligent company that reminded her of England.

William's move to the magnificent Proprietary House, with its marble floors, rich paneling, and stables for twelve carriage horses, combined with his loyalty to Perth Amboy's aristocracy, finally brought him within the social and political elite. Those who had once spurned him as a bastard now sought the comfort and protection of his official presence. But by now Franklin's enemies were many, powerful and determined to bring him down.

In the short space of the twelve years between 1763 and 1775, the ties that had bound Great Britain to her American colonies had become torn. Colonists had to decide between their own personal desire for liberty and their loyalty to the British Crown. William Franklin remained profoundly loyal to King George III. Not even the pleading of his famous father, Benjamin Franklin, American rebel, philosopher, inventor and diplomat, could make William change his mind.

Prior to its major role in the American Revolution, New Jersey had played a relatively minor part in the decade of protest that preceded the actual outbreak of hostilities. By 1775 most Loyalists kept a low profile as patriot forces seized effective control through the colony-wide New Jersey Provincial Congress and its Committee of Safety and Observation. Together they had taken charge of the affairs of the colony in place of the increasingly isolated royal governor and his various officials.

Loyalists objected to imperial taxes, but they believed in obedience to authority. They preferred to stress commercial and practical, rather than political, objections to imperial policies.

The Franklins debate at the Proprietary House

# THE FRANKLINS' GREAT DEBATE

In earlier days Benjamin Franklin had shared a vision of an imperial union between America and Great Britain with his son. But once the rumors of war began, Benjamin Franklin abandoned the idea and warmed to the rebel cause. It was in this charged political atmosphere, while traveling on business for the Post Office Committee in late August and early September of 1775, that Benjamin Franklin made a three-day visit to Perth Amboy to visit his son.

Benjamin Franklin had never felt welcome in Perth Amboy. When he had first visited the town in 1719, he had been a runaway printer's apprentice seeking a day's labor and a dry place to sleep before pushing on to Philadelphia. Unable to find lodgings, he had been hounded by a constable as a common vagrant and escorted to the town limits.

Now on August 30, 1775, though his ride into Perth Amboy was more comfortable than on the previous occasion, he found that the place had become a Royalist bastion. In the words of Charles Pettit, William Franklin's secretary, Perth Amboy was "...almost the only spot in America where a friend to American liberty is a disgraceful character."

Franklin strongly urged his son to join the rebel forces and their radical countermeasures, offering to sign over his entire estate at once if William would just come over to the Revolutionary side. William refused to acquiesce, arguing for patience and conciliation between the contending parties. His decision initiated a lifelong rift between the two strong-willed men. Benjamin Franklin would later conclude, "I have lost my son."

Benjamin and William Franklin, members of one of America's most distinguished families, held their own "Great Debate," arguing for and against independence from Great Britain as they were overheard walking the streets of Perth Amboy, and later at the Proprietary House.

Most schoolchildren think of the American Revolution as a war between the colonies and England. Forgotten in this simplistic teaching, and exemplified by the bitter and angry conversation that the two Franklins shared that September, was that the colonies were divided by a conflict that was as much a civil war as a war for independence, a war in which brothers fought brothers, fathers fought sons, and neighbors fought neighbors, a conflict that split families, communities, and congregations, generating levels of hostility and brutality that changed lives irrevocably. No amount of arguing would ever reconcile the two Franklins. After this visit the elder Franklin referred to the governor's home as "that Tory house."

Many Americans did not want independence. They wanted to remain British subjects. This was especially true in Perth Amboy, the official center of British domination in East Jersey.

# FAST-EBBING AUTHORITY

As the leaves were beginning to turn in the fall of 1775, other royal governors had gone into exile or had ceased to discharge their duties. That November, in an effort to regain his fast-ebbing authority, Governor Franklin called on the members of the old Provincial New Jersey Assembly to establish a committee for reconciliation with the king.

The governor's efforts came to an abrupt halt when patriot forces intercepted his report to London about efforts to stifle the course of the revolt in New Jersey. The discovery revealed him as an active agent of the king, not the enabler of compromise and potential reconciliation as he had publicly portrayed himself.

William Franklin had been secretly sending local newspaper accounts of provincial revolutionary activities to England urging the British to make concessions to the colonists. Franklin's former friend, William Alexander, managed to have one of these communications intercepted as evidence of "treason," which led to the Provincial Congress directing that William Franklin be arrested.

On January 8, 1776 Franklin was put under house arrest, yet still he continued a covert correspondence with British officials. The Continental Congress declared him "...an enemy to the liberties of this country..." in June 1776. His Excellency, the royal governor of New Jersey, was arrested on June 19, 1776 at the Proprietary House by the Middlesex County Militia under the command of Colonel Nathaniel Heard of Woodbridge. William Franklin put his life, fortune, and sacred honor on the line when he appeared before the Provincial Congress in Burlington, the town where for a decade he had lived and served as royal governor.

In Philadelphia, on June 21, congressional delegate Thomas Jefferson of Virginia delivered his first draft of the Declaration of Independence for John Adams to review, including the phrase "We hold these truths to be self evident; that all men are created equal & independent, that from that equal creation they derive rights inherent and inalienable."

Jefferson's draft appears to reject divine right (which was historically used to justify the monarchy) as the determinant of human rights and to use the laws of natural creation as the basis for equal rights. Also on June 21, a court he refused to recognize tried Franklin. And on that very same day the New Jersey Provincial Congress voted 53-3 to declare independence from Great Britain.

Franklin was then led off to Connecticut and a succession of ever-worsening prisons. Two years later, in 1778, he was released during a prisoner exchange after remaining in solitary confinement for 250 days in a Litchfield, Connecticut jail.

Now ailing, Lady Elizabeth Downes Franklin remained at the Proprietary House, eventually moving to New York City before the British evacuation of Perth Amboy. She died there on July 28, 1777 and was interred under the altar of St. Paul's Chapel in New York City. The Continental Congress refused to let William see his wife one more time. Surely it would only have taken one word from his father to ensure mercy for his son, but Benjamin would never forgive William.

## UNSUCCESSFUL REVENGE

Upon his release William Franklin fled to British-held New York City where he plotted revenge on New Jersey patriots, initially as an organizer of the "Refugee Club" and subsequently as president of the Board of Associated Loyalists from 1780 to 1782.

This board organized resistance activities, particularly in Monmouth County, but also in northern New Jersey and Long Island. They were assisted by William Franklin's old Perth Amboy friend and New Jersey Provincial Attorney General, speaker of the Provincial Assembly and British Brigadier General Cortlandt Skinner. One of Governor Franklin's last official acts was making Skinner a major general of the New Jersey Loyalists troops. Franklin also served as chief spokesman for Royalist refugees in hearings before the British Claims Commission.

In August 1782, with the war all but lost, William fled into exile in England, hated by his fellow countrymen and disowned by the father he still loved and even venerated. The ever-witty Benjamin Franklin had the final ironic word when William Franklin read the line in Benjamin's will that read: "The part he acted against me in the late war, which is of public notoriety, will account for my leaving him no more of an estate (than) he endeavored to deprive me of."

Like thousands of other Americans who had supported the losing side in America's first bloody civil war, William had lost his home, his personal property, and his rank in society, while experiencing the pain of the loss of his beloved wife. He was destined to spend the next thirty years of his life in obscurity as a lonely exile in England, never fully accepted by a British government that turned down the majority of his claims of financial loss. Born a subject of the British Empire eight decades before, he died on November 13, 1813. The dream of a noble family dynasty died with him—leaving a legacy that is historic but without legitimate issue.

# INDEPENDENCE IN 1776

## The Flying Camp

*"We shall not cease from exploration. And at the end of all our exploration will be to arrive where we started and know the place for the first time."* -T.S. Eliot

After sustaining Washington's Continental troops' siege of almost a year, on March 17, 1776 the British army boarded warships and transports in Boston Harbor and set sail for the Royal Navy base at Halifax, Nova Scotia. His biographer, James Thomas Flexner, has called General George Washington "The Indispensable Man." For twenty-four years (from his election as Commander-in-Chief until his death) Washington was the most conspicuous and influential man in the United States.

Over a period of time Washington came to understand the conflict as a test of political endurance, and while he might lament missed opportunities, he played the fox more often than the lion. "Perseverance and spirit have done wonders in all ages," he wrote in August 1775. His army would have to perform miracles against the world's best-trained and best-equipped soldiery, for the Continentals had little else left in their arsenal.

Washington lost no time in moving from Boston to New York City with his wife Martha. Smallpox began to run wild through New York City. George was immune, but Martha was not. While they remained there for little over a month, Martha could not stay safely in New York. Prophetically, in May of 1776, from his headquarters in New York City, Washington predicted the British invasion of New Jersey, known for its bountiful food, wood for fuel and feed for animals. Washington now needed to move on again.

# GEORGE AND MARTHA WASHINGTON IN PERTH AMBOY

On May 21, Washington and his wife departed from New York City by ferry for Perth Amboy. There they spent the night of May 22 at the King's Arms Tavern, Perth Amboy's foremost hostelry before and after the Revolution. Built before 1743, portions of the original 2½-story building survived until 1969, when a fire destroyed its final incarnation, the Hotel Packer. During "public times," when the courts were in session, the tavern was the center of social, political and business activity. It stood on the northwest corner of Smith and High Streets.

While at his King's Arms Tavern headquarters, Washington dispatched eight regiments from his already-meager force to protect the exposed coastline between Perth Amboy and Elizabethtown Point. These were regiments General Washington could have used with the main army to defend New York, but the commander-in-chief felt he had no choice in the matter. It was essential that he prevent a British strike into the New Jersey interior.

The Washingtons departed from Perth Amboy the next day for Philadelphia, arriving there on May 24 in time for the general to meet with the Continental Congress and for Martha to meet with her doctor. She allowed him to infect her with a successful smallpox inoculation, the standard procedure at the time. By June 8, Washington was again in New York, leaving Martha behind to recover completely; she rejoined him by mid-month.

Many years later, in 1896, the Danish community of Perth Amboy would gift a life-sized commanding terra cotta statue of George Washington, the work of a local sculptor Nels Alling, to commemorate the visit of the first president of the United States of America. Washington Street and Washington Park in Perth Amboy are named in his honor.

Statue of George Washington

# THE FLYING CAMP HEADQUARTERS AT PERTH AMBOY

In June 1776, at George Washington's urging, the Continental Congress voted to raise companies from Maryland, Delaware and Pennsylvania to form a mobile reserve. Militias were recruited to serve until December.

Washington had hastily organized a "Flying Camp" at Perth Amboy under Brigadier General Hugh Mercer, after whom present-day Mercer County, New Jersey is named. Mercer was a Scotsman, born in Aberdeen. His life as a medical doctor was a strenuous one, full of exacting and unselfish work for others.

## GENERAL HUGH MERCER

Mercer was a supporter of Prince Charles Edward Stuart, remembered in history as "Bonnie Prince Charlie." Mercer served as a surgeon in the Jacobite uprising in which the English overwhelmed the Scots at the Battle of Culloden in 1745. Branded a rebel in the wake of the Scottish defeat, he was forced to flee Scotland for America in 1747, and soon settled in Virginia.

After distinguished military service in America, Mercer was appointed a colonel of the Third Virginia regiment and then a brigadier general in Washington's Flying Camp. With his regiment he marched to Perth Amboy and was headquartered with his officers, including two alumni of the College of William and Mary: future President James Monroe and future Chief Justice John Marshall. Headquarters were established at the Proprietary House just after Royal Governor William Franklin was removed on June 19, 1776.

## THE OFFICER'S OATH

To become an officer in the United States of America one had to swear the following oath:

> *I (name), do acknowledge the United States of America to be free, independent and sovereign states, and declare that the people of these states owe no allegiance or obedience, to George the third, king of Great Britain; and I renounce and refuse any allegiance or obedience to him: and I do promise that I will, with all my power, support, maintain and defend the*

*said United States, against the said king George the third and his heirs and successors, and his and their helpers and supporters, and will serve the said United States in the office of which I now hold, faithfully, according to the best of my skill and understanding. So help me God.*

When Washington set up his Flying Camps he initially expected three to four thousand motivated men. He quickly got less than 2,000 men from Virginia, Maryland, Delaware, Pennsylvania, and New Jersey, all poised to repel any British advance into New Jersey, but not quite the quick-strike type of soldiers he had in mind.

The New Jersey rebel troops were composed of able-bodied men who were organized into local companies for emergency or limited service. They were positioned at Perth Amboy, Bergen Point, Bergen Neck, and Paulus Hook, from which they could be quickly deployed to where "all the king's horses and all the king's men" might attempt an invasion along the North Jersey coast.

## RICHARD STOCKTON AND JOHN WITHERSPOON

The New Jersey legislators convened in Nassau Hall, at the College of New Jersey in Princeton, on August 30, 1776 to select a chief executive. Two names came quickly to mind: Richard Stockton III of Princeton and William Livingston of Elizabeth. Stockton seemed the ideal choice. Scion of a notable New Jersey family, he was a distinguished young lawyer and was fervently liberal.

The vote split evenly on the first ballot, but later in the day the legislators chose Livingston as wartime governor. As commander of the New Jersey Militia, Brigadier General Livingston was descended from a celebrated New York family of Scottish Dissenters. Indeed, almost half of the signatories of the Declaration of Independence were of Scots ancestry.

Richard Stockton III, signer of the Declaration of Independence, lived with his wife Annis Boudinot Stockton in their Princeton home they called

Morven. Annis Boudinot Stockton was the sister of Elias Boudinot IV, President of the Continental Congress, who resided at Morven during their Princeton session in 1783. Between June and November of that year, Princeton Borough was the *de facto* capital of the United States.

Elected to Congress in 1776 and also a signatory of the Declaration of Independence,the Reverend John Witherspoon was a direct descendant of John Knox, the founder of the Presbyterian Church of Scotland. Witherspoon was president of the College of New Jersey (later to become Princeton University) and pastor of the First Presbyterian Church, Princeton, for a quarter of a century.

Witherspoon's education was the product of the Scottish Enlightenment of the eighteenth century. It was characterized by studying the intellectual and scientific accomplishments of Adam Smith, David Hume, and Joseph Black, among many others. Witherspoon brought with him to Princeton the thoughts and theories of this period, making the college there a center of reformist and revolutionary thought.

# THE NEW ENLIGHTENMENT - GOD AND POLITICS

Unquestionably Witherspoon was the leading Presbyterian statesman in America during the eighteenth century, the denomination that contributed most to patriot uprising in New Jersey, since the Presbyterian Church mixed God and politics. Their pastors preached independence from the pulpit. This religious intensity, the New Enlightenment of the eighteenth century, would seed similar future evangelical waves in the United States.

In his book *American Theocracy*, Kevin Phillips advances the idea that, despite pretensions to motivations such as liberty and freedom, their biblical inerrancy, dismissing knowledge and science and the excesses of fundamentalism, lacked the intensity of John Calvin's Geneva or the Catholic Spain of the Inquisition. In other words, the New Enlightenment of the eighteenth century in New Jersey was less demanding and rigid than in other locales.

With the three great English-speaking internal convulsions—the English Civil War of the 1640s, the American Revolution, and the American War between the States, fratricide and religious divisions figured so strongly in people's choosing sides that persisting threads became clear – pietist and Puritans versus High Church adherents, and a recurrent conviction by militant evangelicals that theirs was the cause of liberty. A self-righteous blindness to compromise, low church verses high church, conformance verses non-conformance, political verses economical solutions, war verses peace—all created enmity, hatred and devastating destruction of families, communities, civil order and loss of lives.

The greatest impact of Witherspoon's leadership to the patriot cause was vividly evidenced by the testimony of Puritan John Adams. While on a visit to Morven on August 24, 1774, Adams described Witherspoon as "...high a Son of Liberty as any man in America."

John Adams could vividly recall the day the debate on the Declaration began, Monday of July 1, 1776. At the Pennsylvania State House, about four o'clock in the afternoon, while he was speaking, the hallway door flung open as three booted and spurred men entered, with rain dripping from their coats. The radical members from New Jersey had arrived and had come to vote for independence.

Speaking for New Jersey, Judge Richard Stockton asked to hear the affirmative argument once more before the vote should be taken in Committee of the Whole. Rising to speak, John Adams patiently went through the argument again, while the opposition and two of their speechmakers made both vehement and abusive remarks.

President Witherspoon stepped boldly forward. His coat was soaked from the rain and his clergyman's bib lay wilted on his chest. He declared, "The distinguished gentleman from Massachusetts remarked as we came in that the colonies are ripe for independence. I would like to add that some colonies (presumably looking pointedly at Alsop of New York who had not yet decided for independence) are rotten for the want of it!"

This agonizing debate preceding the decision of the thirteen colonies to declare their independence most likely typified the true feelings of the majority of the population, and was more typical than the polarizing rhetoric of John Witherspoon or Patrick Henry. In this case, it was as if all the passionate oratory of Virginia's Patrick Henry and all the overt rebellion of John Adams and the New Englanders had melded together in the persons of Stockton and Witherspoon. On Tuesday, July 2, 1776, the delegates voted to adopt the resolution for independence.

## THE DECLARATION OF INDEPENDENCE

The ringing preamble of the Declaration of Independence, drafted by Thomas Jefferson, declared it "self-evident" that "all men are created equal," and were endowed with the "inalienable" rights of "life, liberty and the pursuit of happiness." To this noble end, the Congressional delegates pledged their lives, their fortunes, and their sacred honor. Jefferson had the best of editors in private: the words "self-evident" were Benjamin Franklin's addition.

In early July of 1776, the war had certainly become a reality for the citizens of Perth Amboy and New Jersey. With the Declaration of Independence adopted by Congress on July 4, 1776, war had officially begun. But while the Declaration made clear the issue of individual liberties and freedoms from the king of Great Britain, colonists still had to decide which was more important—their desire for independence or their loyalty to the mother country.

In Philadelphia, John Adams would recall "The bells rung all day and almost all night." On July 9, those who favored independence must have been thrilled to hear the bell of the stone tower of Christ Church, New Brunswick peal out. It was summoning citizens to the town green to hear one of the first recitations of the Declaration of Independence, given by Colonel John Neilson. We have no such similar record of a reading of the Declaration at Perth Amboy.

## "GOD SAVE THE KING" - ABANDONED

Elizabeth Franklin, who missed her husband dearly, continued to attend historic old St. Peter's Church, sitting in the private pew reserved for the royal governor and his family. From here she could see the hand-embroidered linen and hangings for the pulpit, a reading desk and altar complete with matching cushions she had made herself. Here she would receive Holy Communion from the hand-wrought chalice. But now she could find little comfort in church as she usually had.

The service at St. Peter's had changed. The Sunday after independence was declared, revolutionaries took the rector outside and, according to local legend, pointed a pistol at his head. They suggested that he drop the prayers for the king and the royal family. He readily complied.

## THE BRITISH PEACE INITIATIVE

It had been Admiral Lord Richard Howe's sincere hope that peace with the Americans could be achieved. Commander of His Majesty's North Atlantic Squadron and a Member of Parliament, British Prime Minister Lord North appointed Lord Howe Acting Peace Commissioner "...for restoring peace to His Majesty's colonies and plantations in North America." As early as January 1776, Lord North had charged Lord Howe to lead a peace commission.

American allegiances at this time were divided. Lord Howe knew very well that about one-third of the colonists were supporters of independence, while Loyalists made up another third of the colonial population. The last third remained neutral for the time being, waiting to see what the future would bring.

Loyalists were usually prosperous citizens, sometimes holders of British appointments who had much to lose from civil disorder. George Washington would denounce Loyalists as "Unhappy wretches! Deluded mortals!" Loyalists were as patriotic as the rebels; they just happened to be on the losing side. In Perth Amboy the overwhelming majority of the population continued to remain Loyalists.

By June 29, 1776 the tide of the war had really turned, and from the Perth Amboy waterfront known as Bluff Park townspeople could witness more than 100 of Lord Howe's transports dropping anchor off Sandy

Hook. By July 4, George Washington was worried that the thousands of redcoats already "marching about" nearby Staten Island "...are leaving no arts unassayed to gain the inhabitants to their side." "The disaffection of that place, and others not far distant, is exceedingly great, and unless it be checked and overawed it may become more general and very alarming," he communicated to Congress.

Already many of the Perth Amboy men of fighting age had slipped away at night to join Cortlandt Skinner, who was forming a new Loyalist regiment on Staten Island. Washington wrote, "It is not likely that in a little time they may attempt to cross to the Jersey side, and induce many to join them, either from motives of interest or fear, unless there is a force to oppose them." Washington ordered Mercer's Flying Camp to arrest the Chief Justice, Frederick Smyth, and other leading Loyalists and march them off to Princeton. Among them were Perth Amboy's medical doctor. Smyth had been a tenant of the East Jersey Board of Proprietors at the Proprietary House from 1766 to 1771.

## EVIDENCE OF SNIPER ACTIVITIES

The Perth Amboy patriots used the steeple of St. Peter's Church as a watchtower to monitor British and Tory activities across the Arthur Kill on Staten Island. Occasionally British marines onboard a brig in Raritan Bay would snipe at patriot Virginia troops that taunted them by marching along the Perth Amboy beach just out of musket range. There were frequent artillery duels across the Arthur Kill Sound, and both sides suffered casualties.

A Philadelphia soldier was killed by one cannonball, a Loyalist prisoner in jail up the street by another. Each day more earthworks were thrown up along the waterfront, and more cannon mounted in them. Perth Amboy was the closest fortress to the largest expeditionary force Britain had ever sent against any enemy.

In July, some Flying Camp militiamen from Woodbridge planted an eighteen pound cannon between breastworks in St. Peter's Churchyard and opened fire on a British man-o-war ship. The British frigate's return fire

Snipers in St. Peter's Churchyard Firing on British Frigate

shot a hole in the gravestone of Gertrude Hay and broke the gravestone of Captain William Bryant, a fragment of which can still be seen in the churchyard.

## CAPTAIN WILLIAM BRYANT

Perth Amboy's leading families were very well connected. William Bryant's daughter Mary (1720-1811) married William Peartree Smith, (1723-1801) an ardent patriot, member of the Committee of Safety and Observation and a charter member of Benjamin Franklin's American Philosophical Society of Philadelphia.

In *An account of the College of New Jersey*, printed in Woodbridge in 1764 by James Parker, William Peartree Smith is listed as one of the college's first trustees. During the Revolution he and his wife made their home at former

Governor Jonathan Belcher's mansion in Elizabeth, New Jersey. William was the great-grandson of William Peartree, mayor of New York City from 1703 to 1707. Their daughter Catherine married Elisha Boudinot in 1778. He was the brother of Elias Boudinot, the president of the Continental Congress.

Captain William Bryant was a resident of Perth Amboy as early as 1761 when the artist John Watson deeded him a lot between Water Street and the Sound that had been previously owned by John Willocks Leslie. In the *New York Journal* of August 20, 1767, Bryant advertised this place for sale, describing it as "A convenient brick house with eight fireplaces very pleasantly situated on the bank with a good water lot, a stable and a barn and a large garden."

This structure, probably built before 1720, still stands at 228 Water Street, although in a greatly modified condition, enlarged and altered beyond recognition. It is the oldest residence in Perth Amboy. Of great historical significance, it is adjacent to Bay View Park. Its original owner was George Willocks, member of the East Jersey Board of Proprietors.

## GEORGE WILLOCKS

Willocks came from Aberdeen, Scotland in 1684 and married Margaret, daughter of Governor Thomas Rudyard. In 1701 he was appointed deputy surveyor under John Reid. On March 27, 1719 the Provincial New Jersey Legislature appointed Dr. John Johnstone, George Willocks, and James Alexander as commissioners to determine the division line between the provinces of New York and New Jersey.

Willocks owned the Long Ferry Tavern, with its handsome grove of indigenous locust trees to its west, and the ferry rights from Perth Amboy to South Amboy and from Perth Amboy to Staten Island.

In his will Willocks left the Long Ferry Tavern and property and part of the present churchyard to St. Peter's Church. In the inventory of Willocks' house made shortly after his death in 1729, more than 700 books were listed individually, comprising what was certainly the largest library in New Jersey at that time. Willocks Lane in Perth Amboy was named in his honor. He and his wife are interred in St. Peter's Churchyard.

## "SUMMER SOLDIER AND SUNSHINE PATRIOT"

General Hugh Mercer experienced countless frustrations as he sought to organize his command in Perth Amboy. Militia companies arrived and departed almost daily, with the result that no orderly troop disposition could be made. As the weeks dragged by without the anticipated attack from Staten Island, the men became restless and clamored to return to their homes.

By July 20, as characterized by Thomas Paine in his pamphlet *The American Crisis*, many of these "summer soldier and sunshine patriot" New Jersey troops, the vast majority of whom were farmers, had been temporarily excused to harvest hay in their sun-baked fields.

## THE HMS EAGLE ARRIVES

On July 12, 1776, arriving eight days after the Declaration of Independence had been signed, and easily visible from the Perth Amboy Bluff, was Lord Richard Howe's flagship, the HMS *Eagle*, rounding the channel bend at Sandy Hook and making its way into New York Harbor. From his headquarters in New York City, General George Washington would write to Nicholas Cooke, Esq. "Lord Howe arrived on Fryday (*sic*) last—his fleet cannot be far off."

There can be no doubt that the sight of hundreds of British vessels moored off Sandy Hook and Raritan Bay must have terrorized the citizens of Perth Amboy. They must have been close to panic when Lord Howe landed 15,000 of his troops on Staten Island, adding to the forces already under the command of his brother, General Sir William Howe.

As more and more ships kept arriving from Europe in the summer of 1776, the citizens of Perth Amboy would witness 479 ships disgorge ordnance, supplies, and some of the world's toughest troops—Highlanders, Irish veterans, Hessian *jaegers*, and cavalrymen—into a sprawling tent city on Staten Island. The encampment spread over fifty square miles, and was well-suited to protect and support the British base. Clearly visible through a spyglass from the Perth Amboy's Proprietary House, these soldiers were willing and ready for combat.

The hues of the redcoat forces began changing as thousands of blue-coated German forces landed on August 14, glad to be ashore after three months at sea. The British army was primarily made up of Irish, Scottish, and German mercenaries, with more Germans than Englishmen fighting on the British side. Keeping in mind that George III was the eldest son of Frederick, Prince of Wales, and Princess Augusta of Saxe-Gotha, the preponderance of Germans should not be too surprising.

A few days later, after reacquainting themselves with their land legs, some Hessian forces marched across Staten Island and were posted at Billop's Point, one of the most important posts on the island. Unfortunately for the residents of the city, this was directly across the Arthur Kill from Perth Amboy. This action was designed to make the Flying Camp think twice about any sort of attack, especially once the bulk of Howe's forces later crossed the Narrows between Staten Island and Brooklyn enroute to Long Island.

The Flying Camp soldiers frequently harassed the Hessians by shooting over the water toward them with their longrifles. Hessian Artillery Lieutenant Goercke was ordered to discharge some grapeshot on the town of Perth Amboy which had the almost immediate effect of stopping the sniper's rifle firing.

## LORD ADMIRAL RICHARD HOWE

Lord Admiral Richard Howe was the head of a powerful aristocratic family. Navy men affectionately called him "Black Dick" because of his dark skin and the fearlessness which he had displayed while under fire when chasing French ships during the Seven Years' War. Much more cautious in temperament than his brother Sir William, Lord Howe held off invading Perth Amboy, as his goal was to secure New York City and possibly make peace.

Perth Amboy's proximity to British-held Staten Island made it strategically important for both sides, and as a result it was the site of ten significant skirmishes. The spectacle of thousands of disciplined British redcoats drilling on Staten Island parade grounds, with only the Arthur Kill separating them, sent fear into the hearts of the citizens of Perth Amboy.

On July 13, General William Howe sent out letters written by Lord Richard Howe to all the colonial governors explaining Lord Howe's peace initiative. A lieutenant carried them from Staten Island to Perth Amboy, where he distributed them to American couriers. This was done despite the advice the admiral had given to his brother that they would have little impact now that the Declaration of Independence had been signed. By mid-August, a total of some 35,000 British and Hessian troops, the largest British expeditionary force ever sent overseas prior to the great embarkations and landings of World Wars I and II, were stationed on Staten Island.

## THE BATTLE OF LONG ISLAND

On August 22, 1776, the Howes landed 15,000 of their Staten Island troops near the Narrows off Long Island in a decisive move to impress upon George Washington and his Continental Army the need to negotiate a peaceful settlement. But the British Army and the American rebels were subsequently engaged at the Battle of Long Island on August 27 (the first great battle of the war and a colossal defeat for the Continental Army), resulting in the withdrawal of Washington's 9,500 men to Manhattan.

The battle was fought over the entire area of today's Brooklyn and to this point had been the largest land battle ever fought in North America. Counting the opposing armies and the Royal Navy, more than 40,000 men took part in it.

Correcting any impression that all American soldiers spoke with an English accent, it is important to remember that the ranks of Revolutionary soldiers included Czechs, Poles, Hungarians, Greeks, Danes, Swedes, Italians, Bohemians, Dutch, Germans, Scots, Irish, Scots-Irish, Swiss, French, Native Americans, Protestants, Catholics, and Jews and African Americans.

Indeed, by 1781, about eight thousand African Americans were fighting on the American side, with twice as many enlisted on the British side. At first slave-owning American leaders like George Washington had been reluctant to recruit black troops. But the British soon proclaimed that any black American slave who ran away from his master to join the British army would be given his freedom and a grant of land in the American colonies. As a result all states but South Carolina and Georgia countered by accepting black recruits, and most states integrated blacks into predominantly white units.

## GENERAL JOHN SULLIVAN

During the Battle of Long Island the British had succeeded in capturing General John Sullivan, the commander of the defeated American forces. As an officer, Sullivan had been treated well, and had dined and conversed with Admiral Howe, who persuaded him to help arrange a face-to-face meeting with members of Congress.

Arriving in Philadelphia on September 2, Sullivan appeared before Congress on September 3 to deliver Lord Howe's request for a "Peace Conference." Taking the floor in protest, John Adams, the patriot who was to become the second president of the United States, called Sullivan "a decoy duck whom Lord Howe has sent among us to seduce us into a renunciation of our independence."

While Sullivan was addressing Congress, Adams muttered under his breath to Dr. Benjamin Rush, who was sitting beside him, that he wished the first shot fired by the British in the Long Island battle had gone through Sullivan's head. But by September 5 Congress assented to a peace conference, not because they were expecting Lord Howe to bend, but out of curiosity to know more about his intentions.

## THE THREE GREAT AMERICAN PEACE COMMISSIONERS

After four days of debate, it was decided that a committee of Peace Commissioners consisting of John Adams, acting as the delegate from New England, Benjamin Franklin, representing the Middle Colonies, and Edward Rutledge, standing in for the South, be sent to meet with Lord Howe.

On September 8 Benjamin Franklin wrote to George Washington, "The Congress having appointed Mr. Adams, Mr. Rutledge and myself to meet Lord Howe and hear what Propositions he may have to make, we purpose setting out to-morrow and to be at Perth Amboy on Wednesday morning...." Franklin also suggested that the conference take place "either at the house on Staten Island opposite Perth Amboy or at the governor's house in Amboy."

But Admiral Howe had already requisitioned the Billop House and estate with troops tented on the property surrounding the manor house. Here their meeting would later be evoked and enshrined. Of all of the peace overtures made to the Americans, this would be the most notable as it was the site of the only face-to-face meeting between the British and the Americans during the entire war.

The beautiful interior of St. Peter's Church, Perth Amboy, contains a series of six stained glass windows produced by Kempe & Company of London, England. It is appropriate that they are in the oldest parish of the Episcopal Church in New Jersey. The Peace Conference window depicts the three great American Peace Commissioners, Benjamin Franklin, John Adams and Edward Rutledge, meeting with the British High Admiral Lord Richard Howe at the Conference House in Tottenville, Staten Island. When the leaves fall from the trees, there is a clear view of the still-extant Conference House from the Perth Amboy waterfront facing Staten Island.

On September 9 the road across New Jersey was filled with soldiers marching to join General Washington. As a consequence, with the roads crowded, rutted and dusty, the journey to reach New Brunswick took two days . Exhausted, Franklin and Adams found lodging at the Indian Queen Tavern. On Wednesday morning, September 11, 1776 they left New Brunswick, and arrived in Perth Amboy later that morning. There they were met at the town wharf by Lord Howe's opulent red-and-gilt barge, on which they crossed the narrow Arthur Kill.

After landing, they were escorted up the great south lawn of Billop House by Lord Howe, stepping between lines of grenadiers "looking as fierce as the ten furies," Adams later recalled. Howe had deliberately chosen the intimidating Hessian Grenadiers, with their tall brass mitre caps, to stand guard when the Americans passed by.

# THE HISTORIC PEACE CONFERENCE SEPTEMBER 11, 1776

Lord Howe was convinced that Americans could not succeed against the strength of the world's most powerful nation and he had obtained the king's permission to forgive those Americans who had taken oaths to support the American cause. The three great American Peace Commissioners also realized that the Declaration of Independence, which proclaimed that "governments are instituted among men, deriving their just powers from the consent of the governed" and that those men had the power to absolve themselves of any allegiance to the British Crown, was completely foreign to Lord Howe.

Lord Howe, as recorded by his secretary Henry Strachey, made it abundantly clear to the commissioners that he could not confer with these Americans as members of Congress—that he "could not acknowledge that body which was not acknowledged by the king, whose delegate he was"—and that therefore could only consider them "merely as gentlemen of great ability and influence," i.e., as private persons.

Conference House

Adams was quick with his reply: "Your Lordship may consider me in what light you please, and indeed, I should be willing to consider myself, for a few moments, in any character which would be agreeable to your Lordship, except that of a British subject."

The three-hour conference eventually came to an end. After a short row back to Perth Amboy, on Howes barge the American Peace Commissioners returned to Philadelphia to report the events of the day to Congress. The meeting was long after referred to as the "Abortive Peace Conference." After September 11, 1776, Great Britain would have to recognize the "independency" of the American nation if she wanted to talk politics. Remembering the abortive events of this day one year later when he was stationed at Perth Amboy, Thomas Paine would write "Those who expect to reap the blessings of freedom, must, like men, undergo the fatigues of supporting it."

As if to remind the world that its Declaration of July was not regretted, the Congress on September 9—the same day its committee departed for Perth Amboy and Staten Island—had passed this resolution: "Resolved, That in all continental commissions, and other instruments, where, heretofore, the words 'United Colonies' have been used, the stile (*sic*) be altered, for the future, to the United States."

# THE BATTLE FOR NEW YORK

Lord Howe had asked his brother Sir William Howe to desist from military action while the conference was pending. But the Howes now saw that only military force would put down the rebellion. With the meeting of September 11 a clear failure, General Howe again took the initiative on September 15 by landing troops at Kips Bay in eastern Manhattan and engaging the Continentals at Harlem Heights the following day.

General Howe now made New York City the British military headquarters in America and established his own headquarters at Mount Pleasant, an estate owned by James Beekman, overlooking the East River. James Beekman's descendants were to later summer in Perth Amboy between 1884 and 1928 at their residence at 1 Lewis Street, and were regular attendees at St. Peter's Church. James Beekman was the great-great grandfather of Sabina Beekman Forbes. She is the wife of Malcolm Stevenson (Steve) Forbes Jr., grandson of the renowned Scottish-American B.C. Forbes, founder of Forbes magazine. Mrs. Forbes father, Gerardus Beekman, born in 1914, was the last Beekman to summer at 1 Lewis Street.

Despite the intense military activity in New York during the autumn of 1776, there was little corresponding movement in New Jersey in general, or Perth Amboy in particular, to indicate a state of war. Winding north beyond Perth Amboy, narrow roads passed salt meadows and tidal marshes along the Arthur Kill to Woodbridge, When travelers went west the roads followed the Raritan River to New Brunswick. Prosperous farmers, many of whom were descended from the original settlers of New Netherlands, populated towns in the Raritan Valley, many with quaint Indian and English names like Metuchen, Piscataway, Sling Tail (present-day Fords) and Woodbridge.

At the outbreak of the Revolution, the bountiful lands of a peaceful agricultural colony surrounded Perth Amboy. Farm produce moved by wagon along country roads to Perth Amboy, a major port for foodstuff being sent to Manhattan. By 1772 the town of Perth Amboy consisted of about 100 houses. Newark was smaller but growing. Like many of her sister Middle

Colonies, New Jersey had moved slowly from protest to rebellion. During the fall of 1776 it would now have to prepare for possible invasion.

On October 12, 1776 the British landed 4,000 men on Throg's Neck, New York, where they were soon stopped by American riflemen. Then, on October 18, Washington withdrew his main army to White Plains while Howe withdrew his forces from Throg's Neck and made a swift landing at Pell's Point. There they engaged the Americans in the Battle of White Plains.

While en route to North Castle on November 7, 1776 Washington wrote to wartime New Jersey Governor William Livingston, saying that he thought it probable that the British would press into New Jersey. He recommended that Governor Livingston alert the state's militia, make any necessary repairs to the barracks at Perth Amboy, Elizabethtown, and New Brunswick, and remove all "Stock, Grain, Effects and Carriages" from the seacoast to the comparative safety of the interior of the state.

## GENERAL ADAM STEPHEN

Despite an order by General Washington on November 8 to send General Adam Stephen's brigade, composed of the 4$^{th}$, 5$^{th}$, and 6$^{th}$ Virginia regiments, to defend Fort Lee, this order appears to have been countermanded and the brigade, after a long march from Virginia, went instead to Perth Amboy. General Stephen was a Scottish-born doctor and military officer educated in Edinburgh, Scotland in charge of the 4$^{th}$ Virginia regiment. He replaced General Mercer, who had been headquartered at the Proprietary House, and who had departed for Fort Lee. Stephen would later be blamed for ordering the American retreat from the Battle of Germantown, Pennsylvania on October 4, 1777.

Next, Washington, his staff and forces shifted to North Castle, crossing the Hudson River at Ling's Ferry on November 12, arriving in Haverstraw, New York. They moved on to Fort Lee on November 13. Assured by Major-General Greene, who commanded the fort, that they could not withstand an assault there, Washington turned his attention to defense of the New Jersey interior against possible British attack. His plan was apparently to push on to Perth Amboy.

Unbeknownst to Washington, the situation at Fort Washington in Manhattan was changing from bad to worse. On November 16 it was under attack, and its surrender became one of the most memorable defeats in American military history. Washington stood silently on the crest of the Palisades at Fort Lee with his senior American officers, Greene, Putnam and Mercer, as they watched the American standard being lowered as the king's colors rose, accompanied by the music of British and German military bands.

The importance of defending New York City for the Americans had been based more on Washington's political judgment than on any military strategy. He had bitterly learned this lesson from the devastating loss of American lives when the British won Fort Washington. This was a lesson that would soon serve him well in New Jersey.

As October turned to November the king and his representatives felt that the time had come for Great Britain to put an end to the American insurgency. New Jersey and perhaps Perth Amboy appeared doomed for an inevitable invasion.

## THE SECOND BRITISH INVASION OF NEW JERSEY

On November 18, 1776 Washington evacuated his troops from Fort Lee on the New Jersey side of the Hudson River in time to avoid a British invasion force of 5,000 soldiers on November 20. They were under the command of General Charles Earl Cornwallis, Sixth Earl of Eyre and a member of the House of Lords. At thirty-eight years of age, Cornwallis was a seasoned and aggressive career officer.

This was the second time the British had invaded New Jersey. The first time was on September 7, 1664, when they forced the Dutch to surrender all of New Netherlands, which included New Jersey. Lacking any sea power, the simple truth was that New York had been indefensible. John Adams's later

The British on the Hudson River at Ft. Lee

description of New York as "a kind of key to the whole continent" had been right on the mark.

At this point Washington's army had been all but defeated. It had suffered enormous casualties and loss of captives to Howe's skilled soldiers at the Battles of Long Island, Harlem Heights, White Plains, and Fort Washington. Following the retreat from Fort Lee and New Bridge Landing, Washington readjusted his war strategy. It was no longer about victory in combat; it was about survival and attrition. Faced with all of these American defeats, Mercer's Flying Camp disintegrated. Some joined Washington's "Long Retreat" across New Jersey while others fled.

## THOMAS PAINE

It had been just a little over two months since Thomas Paine, who had spent the summer of 1776 in Perth Amboy, departed on September 19 to go to Fort Lee to serve as General Nathanael Greene's aide-de-camp. Paine had emigrated from England in 1774 and was one of a group of wandering misfits and idealists attracted to the unrest in America.

Following the publication of Paine's pamphlet *Common Sense* in January, 1776, which argued in favor of total separation from Great Britain, American revolutionary sympathizers had become energized. In July of that year Paine marched into Perth Amboy with the Pennsylvania state militia contingent of the Flying Camp, which was commanded by General Daniel Roberdeau. There was no provision for a secretary for General Roberdeau and Paine volunteered to serve, asking only that his expenses be paid. Roberdeau was a native of the island of St. Kitts, adjacent to the island of Nevis, where Alexander Hamilton was born. While in Perth Amboy that summer, Paine spent time among the militia members who taunted the Hessian soldiers across the Arthur Kill on Billop's Point.

While with General Mercer's Flying Camp in Perth Amboy, Thomas Paine had met the "summer soldier and the sunshine patriot," the sons of Jersey farmers, who when the British had failed to invade New Jersey's coast at Perth Amboy had retreated to their sun-baked fields and harvests. Now Paine, who had joined Washington's little army at Fort Lee, limped along on the muddy roads with the retreating troops to Trenton and scribbled in his notebook at every stop on a drumhead that served as his desk.

## THE AMERICAN CRISIS

Paine's words, written under extreme duress, comprised a series of sixteen pamphlets entitled *The American Crisis*. Their stirring paragraphs, icons of American prose, hammered out from Paine's experiences during the summer of 1776 in Perth Amboy, began,

> *These are the times that try men's souls. The summer soldier and the sunshine patriot will, in this crisis, shrink from the service of their country; but he that stands by it now deserves the love and thanks of man and woman. Tyranny, like hell, is not easily conquered; yet we have this consolation with us, that the harder the conflict, the more glorious the triumph.*

# THE LONG RETREAT

The pursuing British seemed within reach of overtaking Washington and crushing the nascent Revolution. In his book *The Long Retreat*, Arthur S. Lefkowitz contends that this retreat remained relatively obscure compared to the Revolution's more celebrated stories, but that the full story of the First and Second Battles of Trenton and the Battle of Princeton would not have happened had it not been for this action on the part of Washington.

Paine's "sunshine patriot" writing proved all too true. More than 1,000 New Jersey and Maryland troops, whose enlistment period was about to expire, declared that they were going home. Nothing could induce them to stay, not even in this hour of danger. On the last day of November, when the enlistments were up, General Greene, a Rhode Island native, declared the Jerseymen acted "scurrily," ignoring the fact that New Englanders and Southerners had also left the army.

Washington had much to ponder. Outmanned, he faced the threat of the British outflanking his men by landing troops at Perth Amboy and cutting off the American retreat via New Brunswick. Washington knew the possibility of landing British troops at Perth Amboy was real because spies in New York had warned him of a British fleet of warships and transports with seven thousand troops, reputedly ready to embark on a secret mission. This fleet could easily sail to Perth Amboy in one day.

Washington promptly led his remaining 3,400 men across New Jersey, arriving in New Brunswick on November 29. An early-to-rise farmer at the old Cutter Farm on Main Street, Fords, might have glimpsed Captain Alexander Hamilton, Commander of the Independent New York Artillery Company, as he marched along the adjacent road.

Son of a Scottish father and a French mother, as a young man Hamilton was already a veteran with a growing reputation in the army. Small, slender, almost delicate, with a cocked hat pulled down over his eyes, apparently lost in thought, he marched along the Old Dutch Road, today's Route 514, from Woodbridge to New Brunswick. Four years later, in 1780, Hamilton would be stationed in Perth Amboy for three months while conducting prisoner exchanges with the British.

Following the advice of General Sir Henry Clinton, General Sir William Howe argued with his brother, Lord Richard Howe, to let him and his forces land at Perth Amboy. This was a traditional British pincers movement designed to outflank, destroy, and cripple the rebels before the onset of snow. We will never know for certain why Lord Howe refused his brother, but it would seem that Lord Howe wanted a political solution to the conflict.

The success at Fort Lee had emboldened Lord Cornwallis to further pursue the Americans. He was an aggressive soldier and wanted to deliver a killer blow before the Americans had time to regroup. But a strong nor'easter storm caused the roads through Elizabethtown, Rahway, Woodbridge, and Piscataway (a portion of which is now Edison Township) to turn to mud, thereby slowing Cornwallis's advance. Some elite troops had moved ahead of the main column occupying both Woodbridge and Perth Amboy, and to their surprise found both of these communities deserted. Howe had ordered Cornwallis to chase Washington no further south than New Brunswick, which they did.

While in New Brunswick, Washington used Cochrane's Tavern as his headquarters. His letters to Congress from the tavern reflect the drama and urgency of the situation:

> *I am now to inform you that the enemy are still advancing, and that their vanguard has proceeded as far as Bonens (Bonhamtown), a small town about four miles this side of Woodbridge… P.S. Half after one o'clock P M. – the enemy are fast advancing some of them are now in sight. All of the men of the Jersey Flying Camp under General Heard… refused to continue longer in service.*

Leaving Woodbridge on November 30, Cornwallis ordered his troops to march to New Brunswick. As they entered the Piscataway side of the Raritan River along present-day River Road on December 1, young Alexander Hamilton and his New York Artillery fired five cannons at the British from a bluff overlooking the Raritan River. This gave Washington more time to move his forces overnight into Princeton on the morning of December 2.

The village was deserted, since advancing American troops had alerted the villagers to move to safety.

Washington's New Brunswick strategy was to order all boats from Coryell's Ferry (present-day Lambertville) and as far south as Burlington to be transported to Trenton to aid with crossing his troops to Pennsylvania. He then marched his army of 3,400 bedraggled men to Trenton. Exhausted, the army paused by the icy cold waters of the Delaware and then manned the assembled boats to the Pennsylvania side on December 8. New Jersey was now completely at the mercy of the British.

## GENERAL SIR WILLIAM HOWE ARRIVES AT PERTH AMBOY

Meanwhile, on the morning of December 1, General William Howe unexpectedly sailed from New York City to Elizabethtown Point, where he inspected the fortifications that the Americans' Flying Camp had erected there. He quickly continued on to Perth Amboy, distributing copies of his peace proclamation along the way. After his arrival, Howe spent the night as a guest of British General Grant, who was the commander of the troops stationed in the area. Grant's house was the largest and most impressive in town— the Royal Governor's Palace.

In 1759, as a heroic young lieutenant colonel during the French and Indian War, William Howe had led a detachment of light infantry up the steep embankments of Quebec City. This made way for the army of Major James Wolfe and the subsequent defeat of the French under Lieutenant General Louis-Joseph Montcalm on the Plains of Abraham. Later, during the Battle of Bunker Hill in June of 1775, when the British suffered 1,000 casualties before gaining the high ground, Howe had marched in the front line, quickly learning not to underestimate the enemy.

Now as the chief of the British military forces in America, Howe had come to Perth Amboy and here amended his previous strategy in favor of his new "Perth Amboy strategy."

Having completely changed his mind, and upon leaving Perth Amboy the next morning for New Brunswick, Howe ordered Cornwallis to act on his Perth Amboy strategy and advance further into New Jersey His goal was to disperse Washington's rag-tag army and push on to Philadelphia. But when the British forces reached the Delaware River they found that Washington's troops had escaped to the safely of Pennsylvania. In addition, every boat along the river had been safely moored on the Pennsylvania side in order to thwart their efforts to pursue the Americans.

## SIGNER RICHARD STOCKTON'S DEMISE

On December 3, after receiving advance warning that the British were nearby, Richard Stockton evacuated Morven, his handsome home in Princeton, before the British arrival. He had buried the family silver and other treasured objects in the family's garden beforehand. Stockton, marked as a traitor by the British, then fled to his friend John Cowenhoven's house in Freehold, Monmouth County, where he thought he would be safe.

However, he was captured by Loyalist militia at Freehold, taken prisoner and placed in the old Middlesex County Jail on the corner of State and Market Streets in Perth Amboy. He was later transferred to the Provost Prison in New York City where he suffered brutal treatment from his captors while enduring the poor conditions there.

With his health ruined, Stockton accepted a pardon from British Commander General Sir William Howe, and was later released. As part of the terms of his release, he "...gave his word of honour that he would not meddle in the least in American affairs during the war."

Richard Stockton thus became the only Signer of the Declaration of Independence to recant his stance. He died on February 29, 1781, most likely from a lip cancer caused by his harsh handling while in prison. Stockton Street in Perth Amboy is named in his honor.

# BRITISH TREATMENT OF AMERICAN PRISONERS

The most notorious British prison ship was the HMS *Jersey*. Built in 1719, the old British man-of-war held more than 1,000 men at a time below decks. Even though the British had insisted that the *Jersey* had "a variety of apartments for officers and plenty of room between decks for men," in reality its captives lived in severely overcrowded conditions, and were barely fed on spoiled provisions.

The prisoners quickly became "walking skeletons," dressed in rags and covered head to toe with filth and lice. Racked by yellow fever, typhus, and dysentery, many died in their own bloody excrement. The majority of the dead were buried a dozen at a time in shallow graves on the shores of Brooklyn's Wallabout Bay. Based in part on the bones that were collected twenty years after the war's end, most authorities agree that some 11,000 Americans perished aboard the various British prison ships, more than in all the battles of the American Revolution.

# COURAGE AND CONVICTION

Now that Washington and the remnants of his Continental Army had crossed the Delaware River at Trenton into Pennsylvania, the British invasion of New Jersey was complete. This first crossing was as grim as the more famous one of Christmas 1776, but at least the troops were not subject to further harassment. Fearing the British would now seize Philadelphia, the Continental Congress fled to Baltimore, and remained there until March 1777. At this point American troop morale was at a low, and troop desertion became a major concern.

But on December 13, 1776 at Trenton, Sir William Howe made one of the fateful decisions of the war. He decided that he would advance no further than Trenton and then retire his main army to winter headquarters in New York. He ordered Lord Cornwallis to set up a "chain of posts" in Trenton,

Princeton, New Brunswick, Perth Amboy, and Elizabethtown to hold the central part of New Jersey. Howe then returned to New York City and settled in for the winter at the elegant Beekman mansion. Cornwallis made plans to return to England to see his ailing wife, whom he loved dearly.

The overall British command in New Jersey fell to the capable General James Grant, who had left the Proprietary House at Amboy to set up his field headquarters in New Brunswick. Grant was one of six generals serving in America who were members of Parliament. He was famous for a speech he made in the House of Commons in February 1775, proclaiming that the "Americans could not fight," and that he would "undertake to march from one end of the continent to the other with five thousand men."

## THE BRITISH ARRIVE IN PERTH AMBOY

By December 20, the city of Perth Amboy had become an armed camp. Martial law deprived Perth Amboy residents of their basic civil rights under the English Constitution by shutting down the courts and legislature. The quartering of occupying troops in private homes became a continuing source of friction and resentment. Residents were also forced to feed arrogant soldiers and their dependents, all of whom filled the houses in the city. The British also made a barracks out of St. Peter's Church, no doubt to the consternation of some of its parishioners.

By December 19, the first of Tom Paine's *Crisis* essays was in general circulation. Washington ordered it to be read to every regiment camped along the Delaware. By December 22, reports showed only 4,707 American soldiers fit for duty in the Pennsylvania encampment, a decline of more than 1,000 men in a period of two weeks. Washington glumly reported that many of his men were "entirely naked and most thinly clad as to be unfit for service."

Chaos and fear gripped the New Jersey populace during the month of December. The New Jersey Provincial Assembly dissolved, and marauding bands of Tories, British, and Hessians roamed and plundered the prosperous countryside between Trenton and Newark. Local farmers lost horses, cattle, and supplies of all kinds to these raiders. Farm after farm was looted of needed meat, milk, and produce to sustain the Loyalists and British soldiers stationed in Perth Amboy, New Brunswick, and Staten Island. Jerseymen, under the cover of darkness, struck back with their own version of guerrilla warfare, often burning Tory houses and hanging or shooting citizens suspected of giving comfort or aid to the enemy.

By mid-December 1776 the British considered the American rebellion to be on the verge of collapse. Crown forces were in possession of New York City, Newport, Rhode Island, and Perth Amboy, as well as other towns in New Jersey. Many New Jersey citizens had accepted Howe's pardon and hundreds of Loyalists were enlisting in the Provincial Regiment of Perth Amboy's Loyalist Cortlandt Skinner.

It must have seemed to the patriot citizens of New Jersey that all was now lost. The Perth Amboy Loyalists were at ease with the British presence in their city; even the use of St. Peter's Church as a stable for horses seemed better than a rebel takeover of their city.

## THE BATTLES OF TRENTON AND PRINCETON

Washington had hastily written to Congress, stating that "Ten more days will put an end to the existence of our army." But using the intelligence available to him, Washington planned his Christmas night strike on Trenton, crossing the Delaware in the predawn darkness. By 8 a.m. on December 26 they slammed into Trenton and routed some 1,400 dazed Hessians.

In a mere forty-five minutes of fighting, the Americans soundly won the First Battle of Trenton, without the loss of a single man. It was the first notable triumph by the Continental Army and one of Washington's most incredible military victories. Many historians consider the First Battle of Trenton the turning point of the war. This is largely due to the fact that it was a major morale-building action, and it had come just five weeks after Washington was forced to abandon the Hudson Valley and retreat across New Jersey.

Cornwallis Landing Troops at Perth Amboy

# CORNWALLIS LANDS 8,000 TROOPS AT PERTH AMBOY

When the news of the Trenton defeat reached Sir William Howe in New York, he was stunned. He responded immediately by ordering Lord Cornwallis and some of his finest troops to return at once to New Jersey to "bag the fox." Cornwallis landed some 8,000 troops on the shores of Perth Amboy and quickly marched fifty miles west. By January 2, 1777, Cornwallis and his army had reached Princeton. There he left 1,000 men as a rear guard and moved 7,000 to Trenton by nightfall.

During the night Washington moved his troops, many suffering from hunger and with their bloodied feet wrapped in rags, on back roads to Princeton to capture Cornwallis's rear guard. At sunrise on January 3, 1777, these advance troops under Brigadier General Hugh Mercer engaged Cornwallis's army at the Battle of Princeton.

General Mercer, the senior American officer, was bayoneted seven times and beaten severely in the head. His troops, bloodied and in mass confusion, were in the process of retreating when Washington arrived with his main army. He regrouped the bewildered men and repulsed the attack, thus defeating the British regiments. Thomas Jefferson considered Washington the best horseman of his age; that was certainly proven true on this day.

Mercer clung to life for nine days before dying at the Thomas Clarke House, still standing at the present-day Princeton Battlefield State Park. Cornwallis could hear the gunshots while in Trenton and quickly returned, reaching Princeton at noon, but it was too late; the Continental Army had already disappeared. Leaving Princeton, Washington's army had trudged north, camping overnight in Millstone.

The next day, the army proceeded north on present Route 533, crossed the Raritan River at the Van Veighten Bridge, and then continued on to Pluckemin. Imagine the satisfaction that the soldiers must have been feeling on January 4 when they reached Pluckemin. Here Washington ordered an overnight stay to give the exhausted soldiers some time to rest.

The next day Washington withdrew his 5,000 troops and marched north to build their 1777 winter encampment at Morristown. He established Arnold's Tavern on The Green at Morristown as his headquarters. Here he also organized a spy network and put Alexander Hamilton in charge of intelligence. Hamilton would subsequently visit Perth Amboy in 1780 for a prisoner exchange. For the time being the British had been out-generaled and out-fought.

# FIGHTING FOR POLITICAL FREEDOM

## 1777-80

*"A nation is an association of reasonable beings united in a peaceful sharing of the things they cherish. Therefore to determine the quality of a nation, you must consider what those things are."* - St. Augustine

## CORTLANDT SKINNER

Among the Tories of Perth Amboy was British Brigadier General Cortlandt Skinner. He was the son of the Rev.Thomas Skinner, fourth rector of St. Peter's Church, and Elizabeth Van Cortlandt, the daughter of Stephanus Van Cortlandt of New York. Thomas Skinner was the rector at the church for thirty-six years, from 1722 to 1758. Cortlandt Skinner was Attorney General of New Jersey in 1754, an office he held until the Revolution. Except during one year's sickness, he was Speaker of the Assembly between 1765 and 1776.

The minutes of the Board of Proprietors of the Eastern Division of New Jersey dated April 13, 1776 recorded that "Mr. Skinner now absent and likely to continue so for some time," an oblique reference to the fact that Cortlandt Skinner was with the Loyalist forces in New York City.

In his *History of St. Peter's Church*, the Rev. W. Northey Jones reported that Skinner was commissioned by the Crown (Sir William Howe) to raise three battalions to be called the New Jersey Volunteers. This unit was also called "Skinner's Greens," based on the color of their uniforms. Skinner commanded with the rank of Brigadier General throughout the war, sometimes as chief and sometimes as second-in-command of the troops on Staten Island.

On paper, the Volunteers, like other provincial regiments, were armed, paid, fed, and clothed by the British government. Provincial troops were subject to the same discipline as members of the regular British army and were obligated to serve anywhere they were ordered to do so. It has been estimated that 50,000 Americans bore arms for the king during the Revolution as Loyalist militia, provincials, or in the regular British army and navy.

In 1776, Cortlandt Skinner married Elizabeth Kearny, the daughter of Perth Amboy's Phillip Kearny. Because of his Loyalist views, Phillip Kearny was made a prisoner in July 1776 and remained a prisoner with parole in Hunterdon County. He refused to take the American oath and joined the king's troops on their arrival in New Jersey, November 1776.

Returning to Perth Amboy, Phillip Kearny found his Water Street mansion occupied by British troops. When the British evacuated Perth Amboy on June 30, 1777, Kearny moved to New York City and was eventually promoted Lieutenant Colonel of the Militia of the City of New York. After the Revolution he settled in Newark. He and his wife are buried in the vault of Augustus Van Horne in Trinity Churchyard, New York City.

Cortlandt Skinner's Loyalist troops and their raids into Middlesex County in 1777 made them thoroughly hated by the patriots. A pamphlet of the time described Skinner in these terms:

> *...the most ungrateful man in the world, because he has joined the enemies of this country and enlisted men to fight against his neighbours, his friends and his kinfolk; because he had endeavored to transfer the soil that gave him bread from the rightful possessors to a foreign hand; and because, to gain present ease and transitory honors, he would fasten the chains of slavery on three millions of people and their offspring forever.*

# THE BRITISH OCCUPATION OF PERTH AMBOY AND WILLIAM DUNLAP

The British occupation of Perth Amboy from December 1776 until June 30, 1777 imposed hardships on patriot and Tory sympathizers alike. By 1777 the once prosperous and beautiful port city had transformed itself into an armed camp, as the formerly genteel residences of the proprietors, Perth Amboy's landed gentry, became overcrowded with soldiers. British soldiers were also quartered in Perth Amboy's barracks, churches, and taverns, but these buildings were not ample enough to house the large British army. The king's soldiers also commanded public buildings and smaller private dwellings of Loyalists or fleeing patriots.

In his memoir *History of the Arts of Design*, one of Perth Amboy's most celebrated citizens, William Dunlap, had this to say:

> *Perth Amboy being now in the possession of the British, my father returned with his family to his house, and I saw in my native town, particularly after the affairs of Princeton and Trenton, all the varieties and abominations of a crowded camp and garrison. An army who had so recently passed in triumph from the sea to the banks of the Delaware, and chosen their winter-quarters at their pleasure, were now driven in, and crowded upon a point of land washed by the Atlantic, and defended by the guns of the ships which had borne them to the shore as the chastisers of rebellion.*
>
> *I have elsewhere compared the scenes I now witnessed, to the dramatic scenes of Wallenstein's Lager. Here were centered, in addition to those cantoned at the place, all those drawn from the Delaware, Princeton and Brunswick; and the flower and pick of the army, English, Scotch, and German, who had at his time been brought in from Rhode Island. Here was to be seen a party of the 42nd Highlanders, in national costume, and there a regiment of Hessians, their dress and arms a perfect contrast to the first. The slaves of Anspach and Waldeck were there—the first somber as night, the second gaudy as noon. Here dashed by a party of the 17th dragoons, and there scampered a party of Yagers. The trim, neat, and graceful English grenadier, the careless and half-savage Highlander, with his flowing robes and naked knees, and the immovably stiff German, could hardly be taken*

> *for parts of one army. Here might be seen soldiers driving cattle, and others guarding wagons loaded with household furniture, instead of the hay and oats they had been sent for.*
>
> *The landing of the grenadiers and light-infantry from the ships which transported the troops from Rhode Island; their proud march into the hostile neighborhood, to gather the produce of the farmer for the garrison; the sound of the musketry, which soon rolled back upon us; the return of the disabled veterans who could retrace their steps; and the heavy march of the discomfited troops, with their wagons of groaning wounded, in the evening, are all impressed on my mind as pictures of the evils and the soul-stirring scenes of war.*
>
> *These lessons, and others more disgusting—the flogging of English heroes, and thumping and caning German; the brutal licentiousness, which even my tender years could not avoid seeing all around, and the increased disorders among my father's negroes, from mingling with the servants of officers—were my sources of instruction in the winter of 1776-77.*

Indignant citizens in and out of the city shared tales of woe about how the British and Hessians robbed their homes, often forcing their victims to help carry away stolen property. Hay, oats, Indian corn, cattle, and horses disappeared in the twinkling of an eye whenever the raiders appeared. One shocked Loyalist recorded that "families were insulted, stripped of their beds and other furniture—even of their wearing apparel."

Throughout the Revolutionary War, local farmers lost horses, cattle, and supplies of all kinds to the British. This would often occur on a daily or nightly basis, as farm after farm in East Jersey was looted. Rare was the Negro slave who was not seized, and wives and daughters were ravaged and insulted.

The most battered of the thirteen American colonies, the "Garden Colony" would be the scene of the most raids and counter-raids during the war. Loyalists would invade patriot farms, and patriots would in turn seek revenge against their neighbors who supported the king. New Jersey, although it accounts for only 0.2 percent of the nation's territory, has a Revolutionary War heritage unequaled by any other state.

# THE PATRIOTS RETALIATE

Washington's successes at the Battles of Trenton and Princeton did much to enliven the spirits of the New Jersey Militia. By January 5, 1777, under General William Maxwell, they were able to drive the British down the Short Hills, through Springfield, Elizabeth, and Rahway, and back to Perth Amboy. On February 1, General Maxwell's militia engaged Royal forces from Perth Amboy high on King George's Post Road, near Fords, in the Battle of Spunk Hill. On February 23, 1,500 British soldiers again marched out of Perth Amboy, and proceeded through Woodbridge to Rahway, only to be driven back again by Maxwell's forces.

In late winter of 1777, General Sir William Howe decided to strengthen his New Jersey outposts by transferring six battalions of infantry from Rhode Island to Perth Amboy. As a result, on March 8, over 2,000 redcoats marched from Perth Amboy to attack the rebels in their Rahway camps, only to find that they had walked into "a nest of American hornets" during an engagement at Strawberry Hill in Woodbridge. A final British surprise assault occurred on March 16 at Rahway, where several rebel soldiers were killed, and fifteen taken prisoner.

Quakers in parts of Monmouth County and Woodbridge blamed the Presbyterians for being "...the cause of all this bloodshed." This was a common view; Presbyterians were widely viewed by religious minorities, such as Anglicans and many Methodists, as key fomenters of colonial unrest in New Jersey. More than half of General George Washington's New Jersey Continentals were Scots-Irish Presbyterians, and most ministers of that faith were vocal supporters of the revolution.

# CORNWALLIS ATTACKS BOUND BROOK

As spring arrived, the native dogwood and cherry blossoms went into full bloom, and the scent of spring was in the air. Tree leaves were budding out, hinting at the verdure that was to come. And like hibernating animals the armies once again awakened from their torpor.

Unlike the activity that preceded the Battles of Lexington and Concord in Massachusetts in 1775, the army of Lord Cornwallis departed New Brunswick under cover of darkness on the evening of April 12, 1777. They avoided the main roads to prevent the Americans from getting advance warning from spies. The next day Cornwallis's force, consisting of 4,000 British and Hessian troops, made a surprise attack on the 500 to 600 Americans encamped at Bound Brook.

The most dramatic and intense fighting came from two columns of British and Hessian troops who vastly outnumbered the Americans who were sheltered behind a redoubt—an earthen fort constructed in the center of Bound Brook. General Sir William Howe reported to the British government that 30 rebels were killed, and 80 to 90 taken prisoner, including some officers.

The attack was swift and surprising; patriot leader General Benjamin Lincoln was roused from his bed at the Phillip Van Horne House, and sent fleeing through the countryside in his bedclothes. With American defenders fleeing into the hills, village residents were at the mercy of the victorious British and Hessian troops, who ransacked the town before they marched back to New Brunswick.

## SPIES INFORM WASHINGTON

With the news of the defeated Americans at the Battle of Bound Brook clearly in mind, General George Washington departed his winter headquarters at Jacob Arnold's tavern in Morristown. On May 28, 1777 his troops mustered at their encampment at Morristown and were quickly deployed along the east and west branches of Middlebrook and the south side of the First Watchung Ridge overlooking Bound Brook.

Spies had informed Washington that General Howe intended to capture the American capital at Philadelphia in an effort to cut off and isolate the

Southern Colonies. From Washington Rock, situated on the First Mountain of the Watchungs (meaning "high hills" in the Lenape language) in the township of Green Brook, high above the Middlesex County plains below, George Washington could keep a sharp eye on the redcoats. Here he could clearly see the movements of the British army as they deployed some 4,000 troops from occupied New Brunswick, the British field headquarters, and another 13,000 from Perth Amboy, the colonial capital.

Splitting his advance in two columns, General Howe hoped to draw the American troops out of their secure Watchung Mountain position into open battle on the plains below. He advanced some of his troops to the Somerset Court House (present-day Millstone) in the hope that by cutting off an American force at Princeton he could lure Washington from his stronghold. Washington drew back his force from Princeton in an effort to keep them from being slaughtered.

Nightly roadside raids by the American soldiers and guerrillas, combined with roadside killings across the Middlesex County plains, terrorized the British, thus hindering their plans to capture the city of Philadelphia by land. Howe then began to retreat toward New Brunswick, hoping Washington would follow him.

After two days of observing the British Washington thought that the time had come to act. He commanded General Nathanael Greene to advance towards Piscataway to harass the rear of Howe's army. Washington came down from the mountain to Quibbletown (New Market) and had other troops under Lord Stirling advance to Metuchen to guard his left flank.

## THE BATTLE OF THE SHORT HILLS

Howe was now prepared to spring his trap. On June 26 he moved two columns from Perth Amboy, one toward Bonhamtown and the other toward Woodbridge. British and American forces clashed in the Battle of the Short Hills, which was fought between June 25-27 throughout the Plainfield area—from Metuchen and North Edison to Scotch Plains and the Ash Swamp. On the patriot side General William Alexander, known as Lord Stirling, stood his ground, parrying one thrust after another until he could manage an orderly retreat. Washington, hearing the gunfire coming from the direction of Woodbridge, again withdrew to the Watchung Mountains.

The successful waiting game utilized by Washington and the Continental Army, combined with the threat of continued sniper warfare, had forced the British into full retreat. Although Congress had prudently adjourned to Baltimore, the British plans to move their troops across New Jersey to Philadelphia had again been thwarted by General Washington.

On June 28, Howe's army took the old Amwell Road back from Somerset Court House to New Brunswick, looting and burning houses along the way. The British forces returning through Woodbridge to Perth Amboy also vandalized the area in their path, including James Parker's print shop, the first permanent print shop established in New Jersey.

James Parker, apprentice to Benjamin Franklin, had died in 1770. His son, Samuel Franklin Parker, who inherited the print shop, served with Colonel Nathaniel Heard and was likely present at the arrest of Royal Governor William Franklin at Perth Amboy. The younger Parker's home was also burned to the ground by the returning British forces—how the world had changed since the days when the fathers of Samuel Parker and William Franklin had been friends!

# THE BRITISH EVACUATE AND RETURN TO NEW JERSEY

On June 30, 1777, after burning the homes of patriots and Loyalists alike and taking Perth Amboy Tory sympathizers with them, the last of Howe's troops departed Perth Amboy and crossed over to Staten Island to make camp. In Perth Amboy moods grew brighter and tongues looser, and any remaining Tory sympathizers stayed under cover.

The war now moved to the South. Howe loaded his army on transports in hopes of gaining a hold on Philadelphia. After battles at Brandywine and Germantown, Washington's troops spent the winter shivering at Valley

Forge while the British occupying Philadelphia sat warm and snug after invading the city on September 26, 1777. George Washington was now mired in gloom.

But with the surprising defeat of British General John Burgoyne by American General Horatio Gates at Saratoga, New York on October 17, 1777 and the intervention of Benjamin Franklin, American's most distinguished citizen in Europe, France was now willing to consider an alliance with America.

The two countries signed treaties in February 1778, and France, followed by Spain and Holland, entered the war, boosting the confidence of the patriot cause. This alliance proved useful to France as a way of reestablishing her supremacy on the continent of Europe after her prostration of 1763 with the British in North America.

Seeing their naval supply route to Philadelphia threatened by the French, in the spring of 1778 Sir Henry Clinton had replaced Sir William Howe and had been ordered to lead the British army back to New York City. Under the threat of a possible French blockade of Delaware Bay, Cinton chose to march his 20,000 British troops directly across New Jersey to New York.

Instead of marching his troops to New Brunswick and then to Perth Amboy to evacuate them back to Staten Island and then New York, Clinton changed his Perth Amboy strategy at Allentown. Based on an informant's tip, he decided to forego his planned Perth Amboy route and take a route to Sandy Hook through Monmouth County.

Before this could be accomplished, British and American forces clashed near Freehold in Monmouth County and fought the Battle of Monmouth on June 28, 1778. This engagement, the hardest fought battle of the American Revolution, was a political and psychological triumph for the Continental Army and for Washington, and marked a turning point in the war.

On July 3, 1778, from his headquarters at Ross Hall, Piscataway, it has been said that George Washington wrote the "inaugural order for the United States Army to celebrate the 4th of July." At New Brunswick, Washington ordered that the second anniversary of national independence be celebrated with a wave-like firing of muskets and a grand review. Thirteen cannon, one for each colony, boomed and echoed throughout the area, and gunshots could be heard as far as Perth Amboy. This was the first organized celebration of the nation's independence.

Using a spyglass from the Perth Amboy bluff, residents could see the British ships fourteen miles across Raritan Bay evacuating their forces from Sandy Hook to New York City. And since the First and Second British Brigades were shipped to Staten Island at the same time, the cause of American political independence had received a giant boost.

## EVENTS OF 1779

Following the Battle of Monmouth, Washington anticipated that the next major thrust by the British from their New York stronghold would be northward. He positioned his army in a series of camps that crossed from Somerset County, New Jersey to Danbury, Connecticut, to detect and respond to any British forays toward Philadelphia, Albany, or New England. He then positioned his main army of 10,000 troops in Somerset County, New Jersey for the Second Middlebrook Encampment between December 11, 1778 and June 3, 1779. With his forces better prepared to engage them if they decided to move, his strategy was to convince the British not to do so.

The winter and spring of 1779 passed quietly. Threats of an enemy attack on West Point pulled the Americans out of Middlebrook on June 3, 1779 for a forced march to the Hudson River. But the attack never materialized. With Washington absent from New Jersey, Lieutenant Colonel John Graves Simcoe, Commander of Clinton's elite Queen's Rangers, and later first Lieutenant Governor of Upper Canada, staged a terrifying raid on October 25, 1779.

Simcoe's Night-time Capture

# SIMCOE'S RAID

Perth Amboy residents were among the first to hear the hoofbeats of Simcoe and his raiders' horses after they crossed from Staten Island in the darkness of night and pounded through the Raritan River Valley in a dash that most historians have labeled the most daring single event of the war. He and his rangers covered fifty-five miles in a single night, and in the process burned the Somerset County Court House at Millstone. Simcoe was captured by regiment commander John Neilson outside the City of New Brunswick, but the majority of his Rangers made it to back to safety as they swept into South Amboy and crossed over to Staten Island in boats.

With the close of an uneventful 1779 summer campaign, Washington again selected Morristown as the site for his troops' winter encampment. From the heights near the town he could keep a watchful eye on the British in New York City, and be in a position to move his soldiers over well-guarded routes to either the Hudson or Delaware Rivers. The several divisions of his army constructed log huts in an area called Jockey Hollow, three miles southwest of town, while Washington and his official family occupied the Ford mansion on the outskirts of Morristown. The prospect of ultimate victory seemed distant.

## ALEXANDER HAMILTON

During that winter Alexander Hamilton worked in a log cabin office annexed to Washington's Headquarters at the Ford family mansion. The elements conspired against the Continental Army. The weather was the most severe since 1755, and much worse than the winter of 1778, when the troops had been encamped at Valley Forge. The ice froze so thick on New York Bay that the British Army was able to wheel heavy artillery across to New Jersey.

The Arthur Kill, the Raritan River and Raritan Bay also froze solid. Twenty-eight snowstorms pounded the region, including a January blizzard lasting for three days that piled snow in six-foot-high banks. The streets of Perth Amboy were impassable for weeks, and it seemed as if the thick ice on Raritan Bay would never thaw out.

When meeting with other prominent members of the Continental Congress in 1782-83, and later during the Constitutional Convention of 1787, Alexander Hamilton would think back to the warmth of his island birthplace—the British West Indies Isle of Nevis—and contrast it with that bitter winter of 1780. The cold was so intense and so prolonged that streams froze solid, and local mills could not grind grain for the starving troops. Ill-clad soldiers, lacking the barest of protection from the cold, and with icy hands and feet, experienced more cruel privations by far than did those who served with Washington at Valley Forge.

When the winter finally gave way to spring, one can only imagine the relief that Hamilton must have felt when he left Morristown in early March of 1780 to negotiate a prisoner exchange with the British in the city of Perth Amboy.

Hamilton could never have guessed that twenty-four years later (after his fatal duel with U.S. Vice President Aaron Burr Jr. on July 11, 1804), Burr would seek refuge in Perth Amboy at the Commodore Thomas Truxton House called Pleasant View. Overlooking Raritan Bay on Water Street, this was the same residence that Royal Governor Robert Hunter had once occupied.

# AMERICAN VICTORY IN SIGHT

*"The man who never alters his opinion is like standing water, and breeds reptiles of the mind."* - William Blake

With the memories of British raids on New Jersey from Staten Island in June 1780 during the First and Second Battles of Springfield and the successes of British General Sir Henry Clinton in the Southern Campaign at Savannah, Charleston, King's Mountain, and Cowpens, Washington contemplated one of his boldest gambles of all. It took place in August of 1781.

Leaving behind only a few regiments to monitor the large British garrison in New York City, Washington and his French ally, the Comte de Rochambeau, led a combined force of 7,000 American and French soldiers to Yorktown, Virginia. There they trapped the British army of Lord Cornwallis on the Yorktown peninsula. The French fleet arrived just in time to block British rescue ships from entering the Chesapeake Bay.

## CORNWALLIS SURRENDERS AT YORKTOWN

Cornwallis surrendered his army of some 7,000 soldiers and 900 seamen on October 19, 1781. Suitable to the occasion the British bands played "The World Turned Upside Down," a standard English ballad. When the British Prime Minister, Lord North received the news of defeat in London on November 25, 1781, he exclaimed "Oh God! It's all over."

The war was over, but yet it was not over, since it actually continued for several more months. New Jersey Loyalist activities persisted and, stimulated by William Franklin's Board of Associated Loyalists, increased in bitterness and cruelty. They reached a climax in the spring of 1782 in the hanging of Captain Joshua Huddy, commander of a blockhouse at Toms River, in pretended retaliation for the murder of a Loyalist who had been killed after Huddy's capture.

By March 1782, with the resignation of Lord North, a new administration in London was more willing to yield to American demands. The provisional draft of a peace treaty was signed at Paris on November 30, 1782. However, it was not until September 3, 1783 that the final documents were signed, freeing the thirteen colonies from the bonds of Great Britain forever.

In the pandemonium of evacuating New York City, Loyalist William Franklin sold his furniture and prepared to sail for England. He was disgusted with America, and disheartened by British generals who made no secret of their scorn for all Americans. Twenty years after the king had appointed him to his position as royal governor, he sailed from New York for England on August 13, 1782. He never returned to America.

As the preliminary treaty was sped across the Atlantic Ocean for ratification by Congress, the first shiploads of Loyalist refugees began to clear New York and Charleston Harbors for England, Nova Scotia, or the St. John River in New Brunswick, Canada, as well as the Caribbean. This was the result of their petition to the British government to resettle them after the war ended.

A vast migration took more than 100,000 Americans (more than five percent of the population) into exile, probably the highest refugee rate of any revolution. In one day alone, on April 26, 1783, more than 7,000 of them sailed from New York harbor.

## PATRIOT MOBS SEEK REVENGE

As wealthy Loyalists liquidated their assets—their homes in town and country, along with furniture and other belongings—Perth Amboy became a magnet for patriot thieves. Patriot and departing Loyalist alike destroyed nine-tenths of the city. Many had lost their land, possessions, and livelihoods to the rebels. Patriot mobs surged through the streets avenging the ills of a war they blamed on their damned Tory brothers.

Like the few remaining giant English elms of this New Jersey capital, only a few of the important sites of the important colonial years of the city of Perth Amboy remain. Architectural historians estimate that only five percent of the structures that stood in New Jersey in the eighteenth century are still standing today. In Perth Amboy that percentage is much less, since almost all of colonial Perth Amboy is gone. Except for Hudson County, no New Jersey county has as little left as Middlesex.

Washington issued a cease fire on April 9, 1783, thus ending the hostilities. When Congress proclaimed the war's end on April 15, New Jersey church bells summoned their congregations together in thanksgiving six years and 300 days after the arrest of William Franklin, the last Royal Governor of New Jersey.

Soldiers marching across the Jersey midlands from 1776 to 1781 had wasted fields, torched homes, churches, and barns, and generally terrorized the citizenry. Weed-covered ruins of buildings from the British occupation of 1776-77 were in evidence everywhere.

In the spring of 1783, the Continental Congress, struggling with the burden of war debts, was driven from Philadelphia by the threat of mutinous soldiers furious about not receiving their back pay, rations, or sufficient clothing. On June 26, 1783, the Continental Congress made Princeton the *de facto* capital of the new nation until it adjourned in early November.

As peace negotiations dragged on into 1783, the main army, quartered at Newburgh on the Hudson River, grew restive. Congress summoned Washington to New Jersey from his Newburgh headquarters on August 12 to discuss the dissolution of the army. Afterwards, from August 23 to November 10, 1783, Washington made his headquarters at Rockingham, at Rocky Hill.

The Congress was meeting at Nassau Hall in Princeton when Washington consulted with them about the final arrangements for the demobilization of the army. Rockingham is where the final version of Washington's "Farewell

Orders to the Army of the United States" was penned by one of his aides-de-camp, David Cobb, who worked from notes, dictation and suggestions made by Washington.

At Rockingham Washington visited Elias Boudinot, the President of the United States Congress, and Boudinot's sister, Annis Stockton, the widow of Richard Stockton. Other visitors included Thomas Paine, who, it is supposed, had written a letter to Washington that stated that the country wasn't as mindful of his services as it should be; John Paul Jones, the Scots expatriate and one of the greatest fighters in the United States Navy; Thomas Jefferson, who may have demonstrated that the cunning and cruelty of politics could sometimes be balanced by such simplicities as playing the violin; and Congressman James Madison.

## WILLIAM DUNLAP

It was also at Rockingham that George Washington sat for seventeen-year-old portrait painter William Dunlap of Perth Amboy. His painting of George Washington now hangs in the United States Senate. In 1784 William's father sent him to London to study with the famed American neoclassical painter, Benjamin West. In addition to George Washington, Presidents Adams, Jefferson and Madison also sat for Dunlap.

A true renaissance man, William Dunlap is often considered be the father of American drama. He was born in Perth Amboy on February 19, 1776 and is buried on the north side of the nave of St. Peter's Church, beside his parents. In his *History of the Arts and Design* he relates his childhood reminiscences of the town and many interesting incidents of the War of the Revolution.

Dunlap was a friend of the great scholars, artists and writers of his day and a founder and early vice-president of the Natural Academy of Design. During his presidency in 1806, the author of the Declaration of Independence, Thomas Jefferson, shared his notes with William Dunlap on such varied subjects as the "...croaking of frogs in Washington, the early approach of spring, of gardening French and English, preferring the latter, and praising their great taste in laying out their ground."

Of Ulster Scot descent, his family name was originally spelled Dunlop. In the nineteenth century he became the most prolific playwright that America had produced, and was responsible for the construction of the first theatre in New York. He remains to this day one of Perth Amboy's most illustrious citizens.

## THE WAR IS OVER – OR IS JUST THE FIRST ACT CLOSED?

The news of the signing of the Treaty of Paris (largely drafted by Benjamin Franklin) and hence the winning of the War of Independence, reached Congress and Washington on October 31, 1783. The entire nation rejoiced that the United States of America had taken its rightful place among the nations of the world. The last British troops finally sailed from New York City on November 25 of that year. The American victory marked the end of the final effort of a British king to rule as well as reign.

Washington's "Farewell Orders" were dispatched from Rockingham to General Henry Knox at Newburgh, with instructions that they were to be read on November 2 to the troops stationed there. Dr. Benjamin Rush, Signer of the Declaration of Independence, observed, "The American war is over, but that is far from the case with the American Revolution. On the contrary, nothing but the first act of that great drama is closed."

Lacking a national church, a royal family, or aristocratic traditions to bind them, Perth Amboy Americans now would have but one point in common reference—George Washington, who was to become the first President of the United States. It was Washington alone who could pull together both the diversity and the vastness of the new nation. His leadership and character still have the power to inspire, and his life is still worth emulating today.
A pleasant reminder of both Perth Amboy's historic colonial and maritime past and its emergence into the new order is the Kearny Cottage at 63 Catalpa Avenue. It was occupied between 1784 and 1921 by four generations of Kearnys, one of the city's most prominent families.

Michael Kearny was arrested for anti-American activities by order of George Washington in 1776 and directed by the Provincial Congress to remain at Trenton on parole. After his release he departed for New York City where he became an officer in the Loyalist militia. Soon after the British evacuation of New York City he returned to Perth Amboy to retrieve his confiscated 14-acre lot and build his "Cottage" on High Street.

Kearny Cottage

He and his wife, Elizabeth Lawrence Kearny, had been married in 1774. She had remained behind while her husband was in New York. At the Kearny Cottage they raised both their family and Elizabeth's half-brother, seventeen years her junior. His name was James Lawrence and he is remembered in history as Captain James Lawrence who commanded the American frigate *Chesapeake*. It engaged the British ship *Shannon* in the War of 1812, and Lawrence was mortally wounded. While being carried below deck, he ordered "Don't Give Up the Ship!" It became the battle cry of the fleet.

Michael and Elizabeth's youngest son was Commodore Lawrence Kearny. When not otherwise at sea, the Kearny Cottage was his lifelong home. He was the sailor-diplomat responsible for initiating relations between the U.S. and China in the early 1840s. He, his wife Josephine, and sons James Lawrence and John Michael are interred in St. Peter's Churchyard, as are his parents Michael and Elizabeth, along with many Kearny ancestors and descendants.

As with many of Perth Amboy Loyalist families who chose to remain in the new United States, they found a way to meet the challenge of a new order and contribute to the future of their city and country. By 1809, about the time Thomas Jefferson was completing his second term as President, Perth Amboy had made a partial recovery from the devastation of the American Revolution. Always overshadowed by New York as a commercial port and one of the great cities of the New World, Perth Amboy failed to become the great metropolis envisioned by its Scots Proprietors, but its legacy in the struggle for American religious and political independence will always remain.

The original city seal, very much treasured and still owned by the city of Perth Amboy, describes this dream with its image of a ship riding at anchor in the harbor, with the words "Portus Optimus, " or port of opportunity, underneath. The city was destined to become a fashionable nineteenth-century summer resort, still benefiting from its rare combination of natural and historic assets. The bay, with its opportunities for shipbuilding, yachting, and commercial oyster farming, together with a livable historic core, all strengthened the city's nineteenth-century transition.

Strolling along Perth Amboy's waterfront today, one may view many signs describing the New Jersey Coastal Heritage Trail. As with other parts of New Jersey, there is more that makes up Perth Amboy than the stereotypical fleeting impressions of industry. Beginning in the capital city of Perth Amboy, and all along the Coastal Heritage Trail, stretching nearly 300 miles along the Jersey coast, are stories of Lenape Indians, tall ships, historic sites, lighthouses, and a young state that fought for American independence.

# CONCLUSION

*"Nothing then is unchangeable but the inherent and inalienable rights of man."* -Thomas Jefferson

Since the end of the Middle Ages European and American history has been the history of the full emergence of the individual, a process that started in Italy during the Renaissance. A new concept of freedom, which found an ideological expression in the new religious doctrines of religious freedom and moral principles, is most apparent in the Protestant Reformation. Today we realize more and more the democratic principle that no one should be allowed to starve, that society is responsible for all of its members, that no one should be frightened into submission and lose his pride through fear of unemployment, and that freedom of religion is a personal choice.

The principles of economic liberalism, political democracy, religious autonomy, and individualism in personal life gave expression to a longing for freedom, and at the same time seemed to bring mankind nearer to its realization. American history, and in particular New Jersey history as experienced in colonial Perth Amboy, had proven that it was possible for man to govern himself, to make decisions for himself, and to think and feel as he saw fit. The Revolution had overturned the old order.

The fundamental achievements of modern democracy—representative government, that is, government elected by the people and responsible to the people—found a voice when, in 1789, New Jersey became the first state to ratify the Bill of Rights, enumerating the individual freedoms guaranteed to every citizen.

Perth Amboy's and New Jersey's past reticence to glorify the city's past, in preference for the popular patriot colonial locations such as Morristown, Trenton, or sites in Monmouth and Somerset counties, may have had its roots in local history. Perth Amboy society had suffered a profound schism during the course of the war, when factions with histories of disagreements aligned themselves with the patriot or Loyalist camps in an effort to settle old scores.

With brazenly dishonorable acts and severe retaliation on both sides throughout New Jersey, it is remarkable that the populace transitioned into a normal peacetime way of life, continuing on an American journey of hope.

# BIBLIOGRAPHY

## BOOKS


Barber, John W., and Henry Howe. *Historical Collections of the* State *of New Jersey.* Newark, N.J.: Benjamin Olds for Justus H. Bradley, 1844.

Bemis, Samuel Flagg. *A Diplomatic History of the United States.* New York, N.Y.: Henry Holt and Company, 1955.

Berkin, Carol. *Revolutionary Mothers: Women in the Struggle for American Independence.* New York, N.Y.: Alfred A. Knopf, 2005.

Bill, Alfred Hoyt. *New Jersey and the Revolutionary War.* New Brunswick, N.J.: Rutgers University Press, 1964.

Bowen, Catherine Drinker. *John Adams and the American Revolution.* Boston, M.A.: Little, Brown and Company, 1950.

Brady, Patricia. *Martha Washington: An American Life.* New York, N.Y.: Penguin Books, 2006.

Birkner, Michael J., and Paul A. Stellhorn. *The Governors of New Jersey.* Trenton, N.J.: New Jersey Historical Commission, 1982.

Bond, Gordon. *A Printer on the Eve of Revolution.* Morristown, N.J.: New Jersey History Press, 2008.

Brookhiser, Richard. *Founding Father: Rediscovering George Washington*, New York, N.Y.: Simon & Schuster, Inc., 1996.

Chernow, Ron. *Alexander Hamilton.* New York: The Penguin Press, 2004.

Derry, Ellis L. *Old and Historic Churches of New Jersey.* Union City, N.J.: Wm. H. Wise & Co., 1979.

Di Ionno, Mark. *A Guide to New Jersey's Revolutionary War Trail for Families and History Buffs.* New Brunswick, N.J.: Rutgers University Press, 2000.

Doyle, J.A. *The English in America: The Middle Colonies.* Bowie, M.D.: Heritage Books, Inc., 1998.

Farner, Thomas P. *New Jersey in History: Fighting to be Heard.* Harvey Cedars, N.J.: Down the Shore Publishing Corp., 1996.

Fitch, Florence Mary. *One God – The Ways We Worship Him*. New York, N.Y.: Lothrop, Lee & Shepard Co., 1944.

Flexner, James Thomas. *Washington: The Indispensable Man*. New York, N.Y.: Little, Brown and Company, 1969.

Fry, Michael. *How the Scots Made America*. New York, N.Y: St. Martin's Press, 2005.

Gerlach, Larry R. *William Franklin: New Jersey's Last Royal Governor*. Trenton, N.J.: The New Jersey Historical Commission, 1975.

Jones, Rev. W. Northey. *The History of St. Peter's Church*. Perth Amboy, N.J.: 1924.

Karasik, Gary. *New Brunswick and Middlesex County*. Northridge, CA: Windsor Publications, Inc., 1986.

Kler, Joseph H. *God's Happy Cluster, 1688-1963*. Bound Brook, N.J., 1963.

Landsman, Ned C. *Scotland and Its First American Colony, 1683-1765*. Princeton, N.J.: Princeton University Press, 1985.

Lefkowitz, Arthur S. *The Long Retreat: The Calamitous American Defense of New Jersey, 1776*. New Brunswick, N.J.: Rutgers University Press, 1998.

Link, Arthur S., ed. *The First Presbyterian Church of Princeton, Two Centuries of History*. Princeton: The First Presbyterian Church, 1967.

Lurie, Maxine N. and Marc Mappen, eds. *Encyclopedia of New Jersey*. New Brunswick, N.J.: Rutgers University Press, 2004.

----- and Joanne R. Walroth, eds. *The Minutes of the Board of Proprietors of the Eastern Division of New Jersey from 1764 to 1794, Volume IV*. Newark, N.J.: New Jersey Historical Society, 1985.

Matthews, Prich. *Bedminster Township: 250 Years, 1749-1999*. Bedminster, N.J.: Township Committee, 1999.

Meacham, Jon. *Thomas Jefferson: The Art Of Power*. New York, N.Y.: Random House, 2012.

McCullough, David. *John Adams*. New York, N.Y.: Simon and Schuster, 2001.

----- *1776*. New York, N.Y.: Simon and Schuster, 2005.

McCormick, Richard P. *New Jersey from Colony to State: 1609 – 17*89. Princeton, N.J.: D. Van Nostrand Company, Inc., 1964.

McGinnis, William C. *History of Perth Amboy 1651-1960,* Volume III. Perth Amboy, N.J.: American Publishing Company, 1960.

McGuire, Thomas J. *Stop the Revolution*. Mechanicsburg, P.A..: Stackpole Books, 2011.

Miers, Earl Schenck. *Where the Raritan Flows*. New Brunswick, N.J.: Rutgers University Press, 1964.

Miller, George J. *The Minutes of the Board of Proprietors of the Eastern Division of New Jersey from 1685 to 1705*. New York, N.Y.: J. J. Little & Ives Co., 1949.

Mills, W. Jay. *Historic Houses of New Jersey*. Union City, N.J.: William H. Wise & Co., Inc., 1977.

Peck, Donald Johnstone. *A Spirited War*. Franklin, TN.: American History Imprints, 2009.

Phillips, Kevin. *American Theocracy*. New York, N.Y.: Viking, 2006.

Pomfret, John E. *The Province of East New Jersey 1609-1702*. Princeton, N.J.: Princeton University Press, 1962.

Randall, Willard Sterne. *A little Revenge: Benjamin Franklin and His Son.* Boston, MA: Little, Brown and Co., 1984.

----- *Alexander Hamilton*. New York, N.Y.: Harper Collins Publishers, 2003.

-----*The Proprietary House in Amboy*. Perth Amboy, N.J., Proprietary House Association, 1975.

Randall, Willard Sterne, and Nancy Nahra. *Forgotten Americans.* Cambridge, MA.: Perseus Publishing, 1999.

Schimizzi, Ernest and Gregory Schimizzi. *The Staten Island Peace Conference: September 11, 1776*. Albany, N.Y.: New York State American Revolution Bicentennial Commission, 1976.

Shipley, F. Alexander, Robin J. Shipley, and Laura A. Bragdon. *Rediscovery of Rahway*. Self-published, 1976.

Smith, Goldwin. *A Constitutional and Legal History of England*. New York, N.Y.: Charles Scribner's Sons, 1955.

Stellhorn, Paul A., and Michael J. Birkner, eds. *The Governors of New Jersey, 1664-1974*. Trenton, N.J.: New Jersey Historical Commission, 1982.

Thomann, G., *Colonial Liquor Laws: Part II of "Liquor laws of the United States; Their Spirit and Effect."* New York: The United States Brewers Association, 1887.

Veit, Richard F., and Mark Nonestied. *New Jersey Cemeteries and Tombstones*. New Brunswick, N.J.: Rutgers University Press, 2008.

Wall, John P, and Harold E. Pickersgill, eds. *History of Middlesex County, New Jersey - 1664-1920,* Vols I and II. New York, N.Y.: Lewis Historical Publishing Company, Inc., 1921.

Whitehead, William A. *Contributions to the Early History of Perth Amboy and Adjoining Country with Sketches of Men and Events in New Jersey During the Provincial Era*. New York: D. Appleton & Company, 1856.

Wodrow, Robert. *The History of the sufferings of the Church of Scotland from the restoration to the revolution.* Glasgow: Blackie, Fullerten & Co., 1828-30.

# BOOKLETS

Aumack, Douglas and Mark Nonestied. *"The Lost Histories of Perth Amboy."* Middlesex County Cultural and Heritage Commission and the Middlesex County Board of Chosen Freeholders. County of Middlesex New Jersey. 2012.

# MONOGRAPHS

Gerlach, Larry R. "*Politics and Prerogatives: The Aftermath of the Robbery of the East Jersey Treasury in 1768."* New Jersey History, Autumn 1972 Quarterly, The New Jersey Historical Society. 1973.

Parker, Charles W. *"At the Sign of the Unicorn.*" Address delivered In St. Peter's Church, Perth Amboy, N.J., May 4, 1929.

Pavlovsky, William S. *"Old Perth Amboy Walking Guide."* Perth Amboy, N.J.: Perth Amboy Historic Preservation Commission, 2012.

Peck, Donald Johnstone. *"Perth Amboy: The Port City on Raritan Bay."* 2010.

----- Remarks delivered during the dedication of a plaque honoring the "*Henry and Francis.*" 2008.

Magazine of American History. "*The Traditional and Real Washington.*" Vol. III, No.8, August, 1879.

# INDEX

U



V



W

# ABOUT THE AUTHOR

DONALD JOHNSTONE PECK is an alumnus of Earlham College, Richmond, Indiana, Class of 1961, with a major in history and French, including studies at the Institute of Political Studies of the University of Paris, France, 1960.

Professionally, he is the President and CEO of The Clausen Company, Inc., Fords, New Jersey, established in 1957, a leading manufacturer of automotive refinishing products for the automotive aftermarket, and Past President of the National Association of Autobody Filler Manufacturers, 1983-86.

Non-professionally, he is a Trustee for the League of New Jersey Historical Societies; immediate Past President of the Raritan-Millstone Heritage Alliance, Inc., Somerset, New Jersey; past Commissioner for the Woodbridge Historic Preservation Commission, Woodbridge, New Jersey; Life Member (since 1972) of the Proprietary House Association, Perth Amboy, New Jersey and since 2003 President Emeritus, having served on that Board of Directors for eighteen years and for three non-consecutive terms as president, and as board member of the Museums of Perth Amboy.

A direct descendant of six signers of the Mayflower Compact, active memberships include The Society of Mayflower Descendants in the State of New Jersey and several state and national historical organizations. A direct descendant of East Jersey proprietors Sir George Scott and Dr. John Johnstone, he is the author of *A Spirited War: George Washington and the Ghosts of the Revolution in Central New Jersey*, and several monographs including *Perth Amboy: The Port City on Raritan Bay.*

# ABOUT THE ILLUSTRATOR

FRANCIS J. McGINLEY has enjoyed painting for many years, from the time when he won his first art award at the age of thirteen. After he completed his schooling, he started working in the banking industry. Well-known as an artist throughout central New Jersey and the state, he credits his success to early instruction from Raymond Carter, Chuck Miller and Col. Charles Waterhouse.

After retiring from banking, Frank was able to devote more time to his artwork, helping numerous organizations with their funding efforts. Examples of his work abound in Perth Amboy, Woodbridge, New Brunswick, Toms River and many other New Jersey communities. His paintings for the U.S. Air Force are displayed at the Pentagon, West Point, McGuire Air Force Base and the British War Museum.

The recipient of a distinguished lifetime achievement award for art by the Ocean County Cultural and Arts Commission in 2013, he has received numerous other art awards, participated in many individual art shows, and served as a judge for several exhibitions.

In 2012 Frank published his first book, *Let Us Never Forget: Stories and Paintings of World War II,* containing a full range of his work illustrating World War II and the Holocaust together with moving descriptions by actual participants of the circumstances that surround each painting. As an illustrator for *An American Journey of Hope,* he utilized his talents for interpreting a seventeenth and eighteenth century narrative with images not otherwise available.